THE WORD ON
THE YARD

THE WORD ON THE YARD

Stories from D.O.C. #166054

ZOË JENNINGS
DAVID SURO

The Word on the Yard: Stories from D.O.C. #166054

Copyright © 2021 by Zoë Jennings and David Suro

Trade Paperback ISBN: 978-1-7364582-0-4
EBook ISBN: 978-1-7364582-1-1

Edited by Yash Seyedbagheri
Cover design by Kailey Urbaniak
Cover artwork images by Canva and the Colorado Department of Corrections

Published by WIP Publications LLC
Colorado Springs, CO 80907
Kailey Urbaniak Publisher

WIP Publications eBook Edition 2021
WIP Publications Trade Paperback Edition 2021
WIP Publications Hardcover Edition 2021
Printed in the USA

Contents

List of Images

Timeline

1. Image of aerial view of Burlington Prison. Photo Courtesy of The Burlington Record https://www.burlington-record.com/2013/06/05/public-meeting-to-discuss-prison-utilization-in-colorado/.

2. Image of aerial view of Sterling Prison. Photo courtesy of inmateaid.com.

3. Image of aerial view of Delta Prison. Photo courtesy of inmateaid.com.

Chapter 2 America's Storage Unit

1. Image of Kit Carson Correctional Center, A.K.A. Burlington. Image in the public domain, courtesy of Wikimedia. https://upload.wikimedia.org/wikipedia/commons/b/b7/Kit_Carson_Correctional_Center.JPG, accessed 2020.

2. Image of Memphis. Photo courtesy of Memphis.

3. Image of Sean Stoke's mugshot. Photo courtesy of the Colorado Department of Corrections, used with the permission and consent of Sean. https://www.doc.state.co.us/oss/.

Chapter 3 Kool-Aid

1. Image of prison dining hall. Photo courtesy of www.-foodrecipe.review.

2. Image of sign outside the Sterling Correctional Facility. Image is in the public domain, courtesy of Wikimedia. https://upload.wikimedia.org/wikipedia/commons/1/16/Sterling_Correctional_Facility.jpg, accessed 2020.

3. Image of the low side of Sterling Correctional Facility. Photo courtesy of Zoë Jennings.

4. Image of Rusty's mugshot. Photo courtesy of the Colorado Department of Corrections, used with the permission and consent of Rusty. https://www.doc.state.co.us/oss/.

5. Image of Rusty on a motorcycle. Photo courtesy of Rusty.

Chapter 5 Convict Mentality

1. Image of Spooky's mugshot. Photo courtesy of the Colorado Department of Corrections, used with the permission and consent of Spooky. https://www.doc.state.co.us/oss/.

2. Image of Spooky on his way to work post-release. Photo courtesy of Spooky.

3. Image of Crisp's mugshot. Photo courtesy of the Colorado Department of Corrections, used with the permission and consent of Crisp. https://www.doc.state.co.us/oss/.

4. Image of Crisp working out at the gym post-release. Photo courtesy of Crisp.

5. Image of Brain's mugshot. Photo courtesy of the Colorado Department of Corrections, used with the permission and consent of Brain. https://www.doc.state.co.us/oss/.

6. Image of Brain demonstrating proper dog handling technique. Photo courtesy of Brain.

7. Image of Sasse's mugshot. Photo courtesy of the Colorado Department of Corrections, used with the permission and consent of Sasse. https://www.doc.state.co.us/oss/.

8. Image of Sasse post-release. Photo courtesy of Sasse.

9. Image of prison day room. Photo courtesy of davesbargain.com.

Chapter 6 The Man Who Walks With Purpose

1. Image of Chase's mugshot. Photo courtesy of the Colorado Department of Corrections, used with the permission and consent of Chase. https://www.doc.state.co.us/oss/.

2. Image of Chase on a child's bike. Image courtesy of Chase.

3. Image of SD's mugshot. Photo courtesy of the Colorado Department of Corrections, used with the permission and consent of SD. https://www.doc.state.co.us/oss/.

4. Image of SD post-release. Photo courtesy of SD.

Chapter 7 Department of Confinement

1. Image of Dave with a dog in prison. Photo courtesy of Dave Suro.

Chapter 9 No One Does Time Alone

1. Image of Bryan's mugshot. Photo courtesy of the Colorado Department of Corrections, used with the permission and consent of Bryan. https://www.doc.state.co.us/oss/.

2. Image of Bryan taken in prison. Photo courtesy of Bryan.

Chapter 10 The Word on the Yard

1. Image of Cory's mugshot. Photo courtesy of the Colorado Department of Corrections, used with the permission and consent of Cory. https://www.doc.state.co.us/oss/.

2. Image of Cory playing the cello. Photo courtesy of Cory.

"For I was hungry and you gave me something to eat, I was thirsty and you gave me something to drink, I was a stranger and you invited me in, I needed clothes and you clothed me, I was sick and you looked after me, I was in prison and you came to visit me."

Matthew 25:35

Author's Note

I met Dave through a Craigslist advertisement. He was looking for an author to write about his life, with an emphasis on his prison time. I responded with written samples from my college newspaper and an admission that I'd never written a book before. Although he received other offers from more experienced writers, he chose to go forward with me because, as he said, he wanted a younger perspective.

My family and I were prepared for a hoax; my best friend insisted that I text her my location while meeting with Dave for the first time. I didn't think I was in danger. I imagined Dave as lonely, looking for someone to listen to his stories. We met at the library. He bought me chips from the vending machine and he made me laugh. We've been friends since then.

Unlike other tell-alls about prison, we decided this book would go beyond Dave's perspective. Over the first six months of the project, I interviewed his friends and family. Before the book, I wrote mostly arts and culture pieces. Accustomed to writing music reviews and feel-good pieces, I lacked experience interviewing the incarcerated. However, in the process, I met many kind souls, all willing to help with my project. As I interviewed more people who spent time in prison, I became more aware of the nature of our media and their prison coverage. We sensationalize certain cases while lumping together other cases without nuance. I strongly believe that as a culture, we often view the incarcerated as subhuman. I'd like to believe this is because such exclusion from society leads to an "out of sight, out of mind" effect. Through this book, I hope to give the incarcerated a forum for their voices. I hope their experiences and perspectives will be amplified and acknowledged with respect and empathy. Everyone has a story to tell, and no walls should constrain a narrative.

I also thought it important to note, some names and gang names were changed for the privacy of those included in the book.

If you're looking for a clear-cut, chronological story, this may not be the book for you. The recounting of stories and experiences from prison can't fit into a neat box. Blurring the line between protagonists and antagonists, prison stories will swirl through your mind, and challenge your ideas of morality. This book explores the stories of those who are touched by prison. We hope readers observe and honor these stories.

Prologue

Dave told me from the beginning that he wanted the book to be rooted in humor, despite the unavoidably grim context of prison.

"My time (in prison) was defined by my fight against the system in the courts and trying to maintain as fun a life as possible on a day-to-day basis," Dave said. "Humor was present every single day, even on the difficult days."

When I first spoke with Dave via phone about the project, I immediately wanted to know what a middle-aged man who owned his own chiropractic office did to spend time in prison.

Dave's arrest was precipitated by his mother's death, his breakup with his fiancé and a heart attack—events all transpiring within two years. It stood to reason that such culminating events in anyone's life would be enough to trigger a negative response.

Dave's mother had undiagnosed bone marrow cancer. His Aunt Donna told me she never returned from a spleen removal operation.

"It was a shock," Donna said. "No one expected that."

Although Dave cringes at the term *midlife crisis*, some might categorize the drinking and decision-making following these events as just that.

"My entire life before that point had been smooth sailing," Dave said.

In June of 2013, Dave met a woman on a dating website. She attempted to rob him at knife point when she arrived at his house. He reacted by slapping her and smashing her phone in self-defense.

Dave said the night was influenced by excessive drinking.

"I was really sad, and I was really lonely, and that is what led to those really bad decisions," he said.

A few days later, officers were at Dave's door. They questioned him about the events from that night. Dave admitted to slapping her and subsequently smashing her phone. Hospital records revealed that she went to the hospital on three separate occasions after meeting Dave. The night of the altercation with Dave, the doctor released her because she had no significant injuries. During hospital visits in the following days, she was treated for broken facial bones, the culmination of injuries she sustained from altercations with others. With no other suspects named who could have caused those actions, all injuries were attributed to Dave's actions.

Officers charged Dave with first-degree aggravated kidnapping for the destruction of her phone and first-degree aggravated assault for slapping her. The arresting officer was later demoted to a patrol cop due to dereliction of duty, but Dave's fate had already been sealed.

"I don't have very fond thoughts of him," Dave said. "I don't wish harm upon anybody, but I hope he's bored to tears checking parking meters and looking for people who are running red lights."

Dave's story may have followed a different trajectory had he not spoken with the police when confronted.

"I was trying to talk my way out of the situation, and what I did was talk my way into trouble," Dave said. "That's a big mistake; but that's sob story stuff."

Dave was released from jail after scrambling together his $50,000 bail. He spent a year wearing an ankle monitor under the supervision of pre-trial services before his sentencing court date. This gave him time to contact a lawyer, close his chiropractic practice and move his belongings into his father's basement.

"Before my sentencing, frankly, I knew I was going to prison; and I didn't know for how long," Dave said. "I knew it would be a stretch. I was drinking way too much. I was living sort of maniacally."

Despite the drug testing, his pre-sentencing days were sort of "a blow-out party," he told me.

During meetings with his lawyer, it became increasingly clear that Dave would serve time, likely somewhere between five and sixteen years. His lawyer warned him that there would be a 75 percent chance of getting convicted of first-degree aggravated kidnapping. This would get him life in prison with no parole.

"I didn't like that very much," Dave said. "I almost threw up on his desk, quite frankly, when he told me that."

Dave then started making long-term arrangements with friends in preparation for a possible life in prison. Dave asked a friend to manage his cash and other finances. He asked friends to send documents to him in prison. His brother became his power of attorney.

In May of 2014, a plea bargain was presented to Dave that if he pled guilty to his charges, they would be dropped to second degree assault and false imprisonment.

His sentencing hearing in August of 2014 was presided over by a judge who was under investigation for under-sentencing white offenders. Dave's lawyer negotiated with the District Attorney's office. He relayed back to Dave that the DA's office and the judge suspected Dave might be the next Craigslist killer. While questioning Dave, they often asked him how many people he killed.

"Of course, as the investigating wore on, they realized I was just a chiropractor who had a really bad day," Dave said. "I'm not a career criminal by any means. I'm not some guy with a double life."

On sentencing day, Dave's lawyer warned him that if there was significant media presence, he would likely receive a longer sentence. The judge needed positive publicity.

Dave was a former city commissioner for the city of Edgewater, CO. His chiropractic office was located there. The mayor and mayor's husband were his patients.

"'CITY COMMISSIONER ARRESTED' is newsworthy, so there was publicity around my case," Dave said.

Following negotiations, the judge ordered that Dave spend 13 years in prison, with three years parole—*the maximum sentence.*

Timeline

Incarceration is a dynamic process. It contradicts the old adage that one rots in their cobweb-filled cell. For most, their sentences are served across many facilities. Life-long friendships are formed at each new home. Dave served a majority of his sentence at Burlington, Sterling, and Delta—all within the state of Colorado where he was convicted—with brief bus trips and stays at transitory facilities. Dave started at a security level three facility. With appropriate institutional conduct, or *good behavior*, Dave eventually transitioned into lower security facilities.

August 1, 2014: Dave was sentenced at Jefferson County Jail.

August 5, 2014: Arrived at D.R.D.C. (Denver Reception and Diagnostic Center).

August 29, 2014: Prison bus crashed. Dave was transferred to Cheyenne Mountain Re-entry Center.

September 3, 2014: Dave returned to D.R.D.C.

September 10, 2014: Arrived at Burlington, a level three, medium security facility. It was located off I-70 near Kansas in the small town of Burlington. Made of concrete and steel,

Burlington was surrounded by an electrified fence. Windows were about four inches wide. Even if the plexiglass were broken, one couldn't jump out. Toilets were housed inside the cell.

Aerial view of Burlington Prison

April 18, 2016: Moved to Sterling, a level two, minimum-restricted facility. It was located in the northeastern Colorado, near the Nebraska line. The walls were made of dry wall. Windows were four feet by four feet, but did not open. It was surrounded by an electrified perimeter fence. The toilets were not housed in cells.

Aerial view of Sterling Prison.

February 21, 2017: Travelled from Sterling to D.R.D.C.

February 28, 2017: Moved to Cell House Five at Territorial Prison Complex in Cañon City.

March 7, 2017: Arrived at Delta, a minimum-security, level one camp. Windows were four feet by four feet and could open.

Aerial view of Delta Prison.

April 10, 2019: Released from prison

Index of Prison-Specific Terms

The following are terms that will be referenced throughout.

Acting real brand new: Making "fish" or newbie mistakes.

Ad seg: Administrative segregation unit. Ad seg is like going to jail inside of prison. Every cell is a single-occupancy cell. Offenders in ad seg are confined to their cell 24 hours a day.

Affiliated: Membership in a gang.

Alpha response: When every available officer in a prison is called to respond to a situation—almost always involving violence or a medical emergency. Officers alert others of this command from their radio. The whole facility goes into lockdown. One cop will remain in each living unit. The special response team puts on helmets and shields in preparation.

Associated: To be in good standing, but not affiliated with a gang.

Bitch: Any inmate who lets another inmate disrespect him.

Bodied up: A punishment in which a guy is beaten on his body, but not his face or head—usually done by a group.

Break bread: To share something, such as commissary snacks, with someone else.

Camp: A lower-security facility with more amenities and

more freedom. Delta is an example of a camp.

CCA: Corrections Corporation of America, which has since changed its name to CoreCivic.

Check-In: A name given to an inmate who is moved either voluntarily or involuntarily to segregated housing because they are being targeted for violence for some infraction. The name comes from the process of being moved from your cell to somewhere safer like segregated housing which is called *checking in.* Segregated housing is also known as *protective custody* or *segregation.* In order for the check-in to be approved and for the inmate to be moved out of his cell, the inmate must participate in an interview by facility staff. Refusal to participate in the interview results in the inmate's check-in being denied and he is forced to return to his housing unit.

A Check-In immediately becomes a rat once he participates in the interview. Therefore, a Check-In is a bitch and a rat, which equates to an extremely bad reputation.

Chomo: Child molester.

Clavo: Food or other contraband wrapped in plastic wrap and fastened to an inmate's body, usually around the pelvis.

Creep: Anyone in for stalking, a sex crime, or any actions involving children.

Convict: A guy who doesn't care about the rules and is constantly trying to get over on the system.

C.O.: Corrections officer.

COPD: Code of Penal Discipline, the state's "rule book" for inmate behavior in prison. Violations result in COPD write-ups, much like a discipline form in high school.

Cellie: A cell-mate with whom one has a good relationship.

Day room: The central portion of a pod around which all of the cells are positioned. The ground floor room in which the unit C.O.'s office, the entrance to the T-building, as well as tables, microwaves, chairs and a T.V. are located.

Doing dirt: Breaking prison rules for the benefit of a gang.

Doing work: Breaking rules for the benefit of a gang.

D.R.D.C.: Denver Reception and Diagnostic Center, the first facility every Colorado inmate enters after being sentenced in the county courthouse to a state sentence.

Dry snitch: Someone's actions got others in trouble.

Life on the installment plan: A life spent in and out of prison sentences.

Feel some kinda way: Upset to the point of confrontation, but not a direct fighting term.

Feezie: Someone who identifies as a woman or is openly gay.

Fell: When you go to jail or prison. Dave fell out of Jefferson County in May of 2014.

Get your money: A term for exercising. Used as a term of encouragement during a workout itself, or as an answer to the basic question, "What are you up to later?"

Greens: State-issued prison pants and shirt.

GP: General principles.

Inmate: A guy doing his time with the goal of quick release from prison—trying to avoid confrontation.

KCCC: Kit Carson Correction Center, also known as Burlington. It's a private prison owned and run by Corrections Corporation of America (CCA).

Keeping tech: A type of doing work, keeping lookout.

Key-holder: The head shot-caller in a facility.

Kill fence: An electrified fence with enough current passing through it to kill a person. Both Burlington and Sterling have these.

Kite: A written communication with the facility staff, usually to request an appointment with the medical staff or case manager. Written notes between inmates in segregation are also called kites. Kites are often used by snitches.

Leg riders: Prisoners ostracized by the general population, who would brownnose cops. They are not well-liked, but still feared.

Lifer: A guy with a life sentence. Also referred to as "all day."

Colorado level I correctional facilities: These facilities have boundaries but no perimeter fencing. Generally, inmates of higher classifications cannot be housed here. Delta is a level I facility.

Colorado level II correctional facilities: These facilities are bordered with one or two fences, which are patrolled periodically. Inmates classified as minimum restrictive and minimum can be housed here. Generally, inmates of higher classifications cannot be housed here. Sterling is a level II facility.

Colorado level III correctional facilities: These facilities generally have towers, a wall, or a double perimeter fence with razor wire. The perimeter is continuously patrolled by detection devices. Generally, appropriately designated close classified inmates, medium classified inmates, and inmates of lower classification levels may be housed here. Typically, inmates of higher classifications cannot be housed here. Burlington is a level III facility.

NAC: "Non-affiliated Caucasian" or "not a criminal." It refers to a white man who isn't involved in a gang. It can be a term of disrespect, usually when the person is young.

On the ride: Associated or affiliated with a certain gang activity.

On your square: Minding your own business.

Owe list: A record of who owes gambling and/or store debts.

Paper-check: When an inmate or group of inmates demand to view the sentencing paperwork of a new guy at a facility. Paper-checks are performed with the goal of rooting out snitches, rats, chomos, or creeps.

Pod: A segment of the living facility. At Burlington, each pod had 60 cells with a two-person capacity. There were six pods for Colorado inmates and one for Idaho inmates.

Piece of shit cellie: Cell-mate with whom a guy has a toxic relationship.

Put on blast: Speaking about another inmate's personal business out in the open—a glaring sign of disrespect.

Rat: Someone who directly and deliberately snitches.

Real good guy: Used in earnest, it is what it sounds like. Used sarcastically, it is the exact opposite.

Rider: A girlfriend who supports her incarcerated boyfriend or husband.

Shot-caller: A leader of a gang or a leader of a portion of a gang.

Snitch: Any inmate who engages in an action—direct or indirect—that results in getting another inmate in trouble.

Soft yard: A lower restrictions prison.

Short: A guy who is close to his release date.

Shower shark: Gay inmates who walk back and forth in front of the showers.

S.T.G.: Security threat groups. Prison gangs who are viewed as a threat by the prison.

Store: A cell where inmates can go to obtain food and other supplies from another inmate.

T-Building: Living structures shaped like a capital "T" when viewed from above. Dave lived in a T-building at Sterling and Delta. A "T" building holds about 100 guys in double-occupancy cells.

Violation/Violated: A punishment imposed by a gang for an infraction of gang rules. A violation can range from something as small as a hard punch to the chest or as severe as death.

Wreck: A fight. "Careful or you might get into a wreck" were words of warning when dealing with a guy who liked to fight.

Writ: When an inmate leaves a facility for some approved purpose. Inmates who have to go to court for trial on another case go on a "court writ." Inmates with advanced medical needs go on a "medical writ" if they have to go to a hospital.

The Yard: The outdoor area where inmates are allowed to go for fresh air and recreation.

Poorman

"But I say to you, love your enemies, bless those who curse you, do good to those who hate you, and pray for those who spitefully use you and persecute you."
Matthew 5:44

Following his first 55 days in the county jail, Dave was transferred to what was considered the "warehouse" of state correctional facilities, Denver Reception and Diagnostic Center. The center served as a warehouse for residents, who were subsequently bused out to various prisons across the state.

This was Dave's first time living with lifers and convicts.

"Looking around, I saw scared looks on a lot of the new guys' faces, so I knew I wasn't the only one feeling a sense of apprehension," Dave said. "From my days in bicycle racing, I knew how to mask my fear by assuming a neutral facial expression."

Dave's first prison job was as a porter. Dave mopped floors, wiped down handrails, and delivered various hygiene-related items. These duties allowed Dave to be out of the cell for an additional eight hours per day compared to the normal 23 hours a day he would have otherwise spent in his cell.

On his second day as a porter, the officers assigned him to repaint cells in the hole. The directors of the Department of Corrections were scheduled to visit a cell where an inmate hung himself with a bedsheet tied to his bunk bed's ladder. The word on the yard was that the inmate had been a *chomo*. After receiving a life sentence, he was all too aware that it would be a life of proverbial ass kickings from other inmates for his actions.

"Anytime that anyone hangs themselves, the rumors are always that they're either a lifer or a child molester," Dave said. "That's just the standard."

Dave didn't want his story to have the same conclusion.

"To be in a room where a guy had done that, because he was thrust into the same experience that I was being thrust into, I actually got a lot of strength from it," Dave said.

The cell was filthy; years of graffiti and dirt covered the walls. People who were relegated to the hole did hard time. They spent nearly 24 hours per day in their cell, leaving only to shower.

"Being alone in a cell in which a guy had recently killed himself gave me a creepy feeling," Dave said. "I chose to not read the graffiti after I sampled a few of the scribblings of desperate men. I focused on painting over it all, thinking that by covering their words I would somehow be erasing some of the desperation that filled the place."

The assignment would shape how Dave spent the rest of his time in prison.

"I vowed to never lose sight of the big picture of my life," Dave said. "I vowed to make something good of every day I was incarcerated. I vowed to never lose faith. It was in that tiny cell with the smell of death still looming that I came up with my five goals. It was in that cell that I realized that the experience would either destroy me or make me a better person and that there was nothing in between those two options. Change is inevitable. Destruction or improvement were my options, so choosing improvement was one of the easiest choices I have ever made."

Below are the five goals Dave set out to accomplish while he served his time:

1. Leave prison in better physical health than when I entered.

As a former collegiate cyclist, he had an aptitude for bettering his physical health. This change was made easier by his sobriety. By the end of his time, he had met his weight goal of 215 pounds through working out in the gym and walking laps around the yard. He is nearly seven feet tall, for reference.

2. Leave prison with better emotional and spiritual health than when I entered.

To improve his overall mindset, Dave attended classes for inmates who were serving time for drug or alcohol related offenses. He also read the Bible and spoke openly about his faith.

3. Leave prison smarter than when I entered.

Dave utilized his resources to the fullest to strengthen his knowledge. He read the World Book Encyclopedia nearly cover to cover. He studied in the law libraries. Beyond knowledge gained from books, perhaps unintentionally, Dave learned significantly from all the people he met who had also been incarcerated. From them, Dave was exposed to a culture that was the antithesis of his previous life experiences.

4. Leave prison with better relationships with friends and family than when I entered.

Dave never became emotional during our interviews except when talking about his friends and family. He told me that it was the most difficult part of prison. To maintain his relationships, he wrote a multitude of letters. He wrote the letters mindfully so that the recipient would not feel the burden of prison.

5. Leave prison with a better financial situation than when I entered.

Dave, seizing an opportunity that arose from a fateful bus accident, used his assorted professional skills and resources to achieve this goal.

Dave's first prison was a medium-security level private prison owned by CoreCivic, formerly known as the Corrections Corporation of America. One day, while en route from the centralized prison hub to Burlington prison, a food distribution truck collided with the prison bus that Dave was on. The bus stopped at the closest private prison, Cheyenne Mountain Reentry Center in Colorado Springs.

Physicians' assistants and nurses evaluated those injured in the accident. They sent Dave to the hospital via ambulance; the others continued to Burlington prison. Dave was treated in the hospital while handcuffed to the bed, still attired in his prison uniform. Dave suffered a forehead contusion, whiplash resulting in compression of his spinal cord, and a few small bumps and bruises. The accident was bad, but what came after his hospital visit was arguably worse.

Dave would eventually go on to sue the food distribution company that caused the bus crash. The settlement money allowed Dave to live comfortably post-prison, but a lot happened between the accident and the settlement.

After Dave's release from the hospital, officers were uncertain of housing arrangements for Dave as they couldn't find his D.O.C. identification number. Dave was then forbidden from contacting his lawyer or family in any capacity. Officers put him in the punitive segregation unit in the basement of the prison for a week.

Dave wondered if they had forgotten him.

As is a common treatment for people in the hole, Dave said, officers verbally abused him. They called him names and taunted him with food. They poked the food tray through a slot in the door and then removed it quickly, saying things like, "Are you hungry, you piece of shit?"

And while Dave said some corrections officers possessed human decency and goodness, many others were the opposite.

"They are the lowest common denominator of legal working people in our society," Dave said of those officers in the latter category. "They're horrible. They're fucked up people, and if they weren't a correction officer, they'd be an inmate. Their thinking is not much different."

Officer Poorman was one of the first people in Dave's life to fuck with him.

"I was an employer, a professor, a teacher," Dave said. "No one ever fucks with those kinds of people."

Dave soon started thinking of officers as a part of the prison's physical apparatus, not as individuals.

"There's no point in getting angry at him any more than I'm angry at the door," Dave said. "When I saw the cops walking around, I would see them as a door, just another part of the prison. I can't let them affect my emotions because I've seen people trying to get into a fight with a door, and that doesn't go well."

Jared Polis, Colorado's incumbent governor, hopes to shut down the private prison industry in the state. Dave called me when he learned that the Cheyenne Mountain Reentry Center was given orders to close in January 2020. We were both excited but also wondered about Officer Poorman.

"I'll never forget the name," Dave said. "I thought it was really fitting."

America's Storage Unit

"And he said: 'Truly I tell you, unless you change and become like little children, you will never enter the kingdom of heaven. Therefore, whoever takes the lowly position of this child is the greatest in the kingdom of heaven. And whoever welcomes one such child in my name welcomes me.'"

Matthew 18:3

Sauer relived his case every day. Sauer was one of Dave's first cellmates. Spending six years incarcerated before living with Dave, he was in for repeatedly beating his wife. Sauer still had an Eiffel Tower-shaped scar on the side of his head from when his former wife struck him with a figurine. Sauer believed the entire affair was a frame job instigated by his wife and the D.A.

"He was just full of hatred and bitterness," Dave said of Sauer. "It was just destroying him as a person."

Prison is the perfect place to ruminate in negative thoughts.

"The guys who are just filled with hatred have a really hard time," Dave said. "You can see it on their face. I never got to the point where I loved the judge or the district attorney, but remembering that they were just doing their job helped me to not harbor a lot of resentment. I grew to actually feel sorry for them. The only way for them to be good at their job is to sometimes compromise their personal principles."

Dave didn't think he got a fair hearing with his case; he refused to let that jade him.

"I thought about decisions with substance abuse and promiscuity, and how I was meeting people—these really stupid decisions that led to a chain of events," Dave said. "I think about them because that's stuff not to have as part of my life anymore. My life is so much better if I'm not chugging whiskey with breakfast. I was not mentally equipped to deal with those hardships. And chugging whiskey is not a fix. It didn't work."

———

Mistakes

Prison has a considerable learning curve for those with no experience. Dave remembers the mistakes he made early in his prison time.

One significant mistake: Coughing without a paper towel.

People with colds were expected to carry a paper towel around. This was viewed as an immense gesture of respect to the entire inmate population. Convicts believed spreading germs was as insulting as someone spitting in their mouths. To speak to anyone before brushing your teeth in the morning, including your cellmate, was considered disrespectful. Other significant acts of disrespect included returning from the gym and going into someone else's cell before taking a shower. Sitting on another inmate's bed was taboo.

"That's the one space in the whole freaking world that you can really say is yours," Dave said.

Taking two showers on most days, Dave washed his hands more in prison than other times in his life. If someone failed to wash their hands, the whole yard would become painfully aware of it.

Getting sick and coughing in the dining hall would be "-like going to church with no pants on," Dave said. "You would never think about doing it."

Prisons were extremely clean spaces. Everyone had a designated job, ranging from cleaning the handrails to cleaning the microwave. Every two hours someone cleaned the microwave, carefully documenting every session. If your food boiled over, it was your responsibility to run, grab a towel, and clean it with due haste.

"With guys who have nothing to do with their time, keeping everything meticulously clean is a great way to spend a lot of time," Dave said.

Cleaning as a means of entertainment and purpose was especially present in private prisons, where morale was low and budgets were tight. Burlington prison has since closed, like many other CoreCivic prisons around Colorado.

Kit Carson Correctional Center, A.K.A. Burlington

Each wing of the prison housed 120 men, with a glass rotunda where officers could monitor all activities. Units A and B were closed for remodeling during Dave's time there.

Dave watched as the company brought in new hires dressed in civilian clothing and marched them through the facility. Private prisons generally have a lower bar when hiring their staff. Generating money is typically their first priority, resulting in high staff turnover and poor working conditions.

"It's like the carnival is coming to town," Dave said.

The recreation yard was surrounded by a walking path that was one fifth of a mile, slightly shorter than a high school track. Two men occupied each seven by eight-foot cell. Each unit received two hours of outdoor time, regardless of weather.

People from Idaho were bused into Unit C. CoreCivic contracted with Idaho's D.O.C. to transfer them to Colorado for their safety. The word on the yard was that they were in protective custody. They were probably cops, DEAs who were caught doing something dirty or child molesters. Their uniforms were Smurf blue, compared to Dave's forest green set.

————

Dave's Best Friend

My first interview for this book was with Tim. Tim is one of Dave's best friends. We met in a cafe near downtown Denver. Tim has a chiropractic practice and started a small business producing backcountry dog rescue harnesses and ergonomically safe small dog carriers.

Dave and Tim met in chiropractic school in 2004. Tim has affectionately nicknamed Dave "string bean" because of his tall, skinny frame. Dave is approximately 6'7" in prison boots.

Dave entrusted Tim with his life savings in cash while in prison. Tim offered Dave a place to stay upon his release and also served as his parole sponsor.

"The guy's my hero," Dave said.

The two formed a friendship, in large part over a shared love of cycling. When they weren't studying for school together, they biked or went fishing at the beach.

"There's something interesting about people who are in

some sort of endurance sport, especially biking or cycling, because you get to spend four or five hours next to someone on a bike," Tim said. "And you just learn them. It's not like sitting at a bar or sitting on a beach where there's all these distractions. We got to be pretty good friends pretty quick, just because you learn everything about them because there's nothing else to do."

Several months into school, Tim's father unexpectedly died. He called Dave first. Tim considered quitting school, but Dave offered to do group projects and give Tim the credit.

"That's what really galvanized our friendship," Dave said.

Tim and Dave still joke about how the biggest trials in their lives brought them closer together. Tim held Dave's infant daughter at Dave's mom's funeral.

"It was a big hit for him," Tim said. "He was really close to his mom; and she was a lovely woman."

Tim knew Dave was going through a great deal but could never have guessed that Dave was in jail when Dave's chiropractic office manager called asking about his whereabouts.

"It was a big shock," Tim said. "Everyone's got friends that are like it's only a matter of time before the wheels come off this thing. Not with him. That's what makes it so crazy is it was just so left field. It's just one of those things in life that's just a culmination of so much going on that it just becomes pretty overwhelming."

He video chatted with Dave at the jail, trying to keep the conversation light. When he learned of the scope of Dave's charges, they didn't match Dave's sensibilities, Tim told me.

"It's out of character, but I understand it," Tim said. "I don't need to define it. I get it. He was using a lot of distraction to not face the big things."

While in prison, Tim sent Dave money, books, updates on the Tour de France, and medical journals.

"One of my fears was I worried about who would come out," Tim said. "How much would it change who I knew going in? I felt like I wanted to keep our conversations at our level—things we had been talking about for ten years."

One day Tim received a large package at work from Sterling Prison; inside was Dave's prison uniform.

"I have no story," Tim said. "I don't know this is coming. Literally, I kinda thought he was going to kill himself. That's my first thought. I was freaking out."

Dave had snuck the uniform out as an act of defiance against the system.

On another occasion, an imposing man named Memphis asked for Tim at his office. He wore a leather jacket and silver earrings. Tim thought perhaps he owed the man money.

"I'm thinking this guy is going to pommel me for some reason," Tim said.

Memphis

But instead, Memphis told Tim he did time with Dave at Burlington. Tim and Memphis are now friends.

"He's a great guy," Tim said. "He's a fantastic human being. The relationships that Dave has made in that part of his life, I think, are going to be with him for a long time."

Tim wasn't a stranger to prison culture. He knew the numerous pitfalls, especially the dangers of racial radicalization.

"Please don't come out a white supremacist," Tim thought. "Please don't do that to me because we aren't going to be friends anymore. I didn't want my buddy to walk out with a swastika on his face. I wanted Dave to come out the way Dave came in. I like him."

Now, when Tim and Dave are out, they occasionally run across people with whom Dave did time. Tim has been good-natured about Dave's new crowd. He seems amused by the juxtaposition of Dave's good old friends and his new prison ones.

"He mitigated that stuff incredibly well," Tim said. "The guys he got out with, it's like going to war: once you go through that you make these bonds with the people that you've gone through some pretty serious shit together."

Tim saved all their letters, which were helpful for me to sift through while working on the book. He saved them for Dave, hoping he could see the trajectory of his journey through them.

Tim is also surprised and relieved that prison didn't change Dave too much. I imagined my best friend going to prison and had an immediate respect for Tim handling the situation with humor and grace.

"I'm blown away," Tim said. "I don't know many people who could come out of it as reasonably amazing as he has. It's not a big switch."

Even behind the walls, his best friend not only survived but grew.

Sean Stokes

Sledgehammer Hands

Another superhero in Dave's life is Sean Stokes. When Dave first arrived at Burlington, Dave stuck out—not only because he was a tall guy with a neck brace from his bus accident. Dave had never been to prison and broke countless prison rules on his arrival. These actions pissed off many who strictly understood and adhered to the rules.

I met Sean at a prison in Cañon City. Weeks before, I sent in my application to be added to his visitor's list. During weekend visiting hours, I drove to the prison. I was patted down and went through a metal detector. I begrudgingly took out my metal nose piercing. Later, Sean told me his teenage daughter was dissuaded from visiting him in prison because of the stringent regulations that made her feel like she was doing something wrong. The correctional officers were friendly for the most part. Dave told me that it's a privilege for cops to work in the visiting area of the prisons, so they were on their best behavior to remain at that particular post.

I rode on a small bus with two other families—one older couple visiting from Georgia and a mother with a young daughter. The passengers kept the mood light. I couldn't help but feel sad for those who have to visit loved ones in prison. The bus driver reminded me of a tour guide. He pointed out the assorted prison programs as if they were tourist attractions. There was a dairy farm, a wild horse herd, and a bighorn sheep herd—all operated by people imprisoned there. I wondered how much they were paid to work those operations. He didn't point out the grim-looking buildings. One drab building was surrounded by razor wire and had small slits for windows. I later asked Sean who lived there, assuming it was the punitive segregation unit of the complex. He told me that was where people who have severe mental illness are housed.

At first, I was delivered to the wrong area of the prison, but the error was rectified, and I was sent to Sean's unit. When I told Dave later about the incident, he was thoroughly amused.

I spent the whole day talking with Sean during the visiting hours. Dave sent me with money so I could buy Sean an array of snacks from the vending machines. These snacks were a treat from their regular fare.

Sean has been in prison for most of his adult life. He told me he wasn't a very good person before being sentenced. He was involved in organized crime and his charges ranged from firearm violations to human trafficking. When he first went to prison, he was also heavily involved in prison gangs. Sean said he is now one of about 25 who have completed a program helping incarcerated persons cut their ties to prison gangs. It is uncommon to repudiate gang affiliation because gangs often retaliate violently when members do so.

Sean's life changed when his daughter asked him if he were going to Hell. She attends a Catholic school. Sean responded that he probably would end up there. His daughter, in turn, responded that she would follow him to Hell. Sean became a Christian that day.

He became a caretaker for people who were dying while incarcerated. He was often the sole person to hold their hands as they died; familial presence was strictly forbidden. Now a certified counselor, he mentors young people in prison. When they express openness to his advice, he helps them navigate their time without gang involvement.

Dave was one of Sean's projects.

"I thought Dave had a funny case when I first met him," Sean said. "He sort of hung around with the guys who had funny cases and just didn't fit in."

By *funny* cases, Sean said, he meant cases that involved sexual assault, child molestation, or abuse. When middle-aged white men entered prison, it was often assumed they committed a crime of this nature. People doing time for other crimes, such as violence or drug use, often started their time earlier in life. Dave fit the profile of the *funny* cases. Sean was worried because he wore his jacket completely zipped up. People with funny cases often bundled in their clothes to protect themselves from getting stabbed.

Convicts, who were uncertain of Dave's intentions, were hoping to take swings at him. Sean knew that if he didn't punish Dave for his disregard for prison rules, someone else would exact much worse retribution. Sean disciplined Dave as little as possible in the first couple months Dave arrived. Types of discipline included telling Dave he needed to spend time in his cell, as a form of prison timeout. On one occasion, the discipline was a chest-check, which was a short jab to the chest meant to get Dave's attention rather than to hurt him.

Everyone respected Sean. With hands like sledgehammers and a muscular frame, he was notorious for beating up three people at one time if provoked.

"After talking with him, I figured out he was just brand new," Sean said. "I decided to help him because it was the right thing to do. Dave was so book smart it made him prison stupid. Just about every step he took for the first time was the wrong one. It was like a giraffe walking around a lion's den."

For the first time in Dave's life, education and amiability failed to help him make positive connections.

"The humor in the whole situation was trying to convince Dave that in prison right is wrong and wrong is right," Sean said. "He wanted to argue the point. Imagine trying to convince a regular person the right thing is wrong."

But Dave became more than just a mentoring project.

"I count Dave as one of my best friends," Sean said. "You don't meet very many people in prison that are deep down super good people."

Dave agrees wholeheartedly. He sends Sean approximately $100 a month—a healthy salary by prison standards.

"That's the difference between having everything you want or need while you're in there," Dave told me. "He's a big guy, big eater."

Dave's happy to help Sean live a little better. Sean also helps Dave with his business.

There is an urgent need for mental health counselors like Sean in prison.

"All the tragedies that people face out here, they face them in there the exact same way," Dave told me. "But they are separated, so things can be very difficult. These are common occurrences. The prisons just don't have enough money to staff mental health counselors."

Statistics vary, but within prison populations, about 20 percent of inmates have serious mental health issues. Dave believes this figure should be closer to 50 percent based on personal observation. Some are reluctant to come to a staff member for help, due in large part to the suspicion of ratting.

"Inmates who are intelligent don't want to be diagnosed with a mental illness because a diagnosis can make moving through the system a slower process," Dave said.

Dave even came to Sean for mental health counseling when he was released.

"Basically, he was my mental health counselor," Dave said. "I said, 'Sean this is crazy. You're in. I'm out. I'm supposed to be helping you and it's going the other way this time.' But that's the way my friendship with him has always been. There have been times when I've helped him. Times when he's helped me. I guess that's the basis of any good friendship."

Sean and I also talked about the broader prison system and his life. Sean has spent time in maximum security prisons but is relieved to be in a lower-security facility now. He is up for parole in January 2024. State-run prisons have reached capacity in Colorado due to statewide private prison shutdowns. Sean is hoping for an early release, due to the visible and positive changes in his life.

During the interview, I met the prison warden. He and other prison staff stood among inmates who participated in a self-improvement class. Students were admiring a mural that a student serving a life sentence had painted on the visiting room wall. The beautifully painted mural depicted the cycle of people who commit crimes reentering society for the better. In particular, the mural paid homage to officers killed while working.

Sean compares prisons to storage units—a metaphor I will never forget.

"We fill them up with the people we don't want to deal with now," Sean said. "When we return years later to check on the contents of the storage unit, they are often dusty and unusable from sitting in a dark, confined area for years."

Sean believes that prisons need to reevaluate their particular approach to the incarcerated.

"Prison does not work at all," Sean said. "It will only do good if they educate, but most just confine. Most people get out of prison worse than when they came in. On a deeper level, prison is traumatic, and we all know trauma does super bad things to the human mind. Prison is crime school and does not work."

Most people in prison lack educational backgrounds beyond high school or a G.E.D. certification. Sean told me that one way to combat the high recidivism rates would be to implement education programs. He's not sure where the funding would come from.

"This is a problem because we only make 60 cents a day," Sean said. "And that's not enough to pay for soap and toothpaste, let alone an education."

Once released, Sean hopes to help prisons from the other side of the bars. He plans to participate in reform efforts and lobby the state government. He likes to believe that if the public truly were aware of the traumatic, ineffective nature of the prison system, they would demand change.

After returning to my car and putting in my nose piercing again, I called Dave. I thanked him for shifting my perspective. On paper, Sean was a deplorable person, but his crimes no longer defined him for me. He was an interesting and kind person. He asked me what goals I had for self-improvement. While driving out of Cañon City, I noticed a large billboard advertising a gimmicky prison museum. It kind of made me sick. Before this project, I may have thought it was interesting. I may have even visited the museum.

3

Kool-Aid

"So in everything, do to others what you would have them do to you, for this sums up the Law and the Prophets."
Matthew 7:12

Everyone in prison had a job. What these jobs didn't pay in actual wages they paid in sentence reduction, which was only favorable for people with short sentences.

Dave worked in the kitchen at all three prisons where he spent time. Dave moved up from the dish pit to assembling meals for people with special diets, such as Hillel or Kosher. Although some practiced these religions, others simply got bored and requested a diet change, Dave said. Meals prepared for people with special diets were often a reprieve from the bland food Dave ate. Sometimes he and others working in the kitchen stole food designated for those with a special diet.

"In hindsight, I feel a little bit guilty about that because if he truly was someone of the Muslim faith, and if he really believed that his afterlife is affected by which burger he eats, I could have tainted his ability to have a happy afterlife," Dave said.

Dave observed cops' penchant for dirtiness too.

"The cops aren't much better than your average inmate as far as their character as individuals," Dave said. "Everybody's locked up. The line gets a little bit blurred. There are cops bringing in drugs and bringing in cell phones."

Prison dining hall.

When Dave first started working in the kitchen at Burlington, others suspected he was a snitch because he didn't steal food. As he became more comfortable, he began stealing food and arguing with the cops who managed the kitchen.

"He's a big comedian in the kitchen with a big personality," SD, one of his friends who worked in the kitchen with Dave, said. "He's very savvy with the law. If something's not right he'll push the pen. He'll tell the captain what's not right. And you need advocates like that. Dave's the kitchen advocate. They hated him for that. He's a very strategic kind of guy. He's a tactician for sure."

Gangs in prison are typically demarcated by race. Workers had no trouble stealing food allocated to members of rival gangs considered racially inferior. Each gang considered stealing food their own imperative.

Dave worked with Woodchip John in the Burlington prison kitchen. Their only tasks were providing beverages and wiping down tables. Woodchip John earned his name after a stray woodchip landed in his eye while working in a prison in Idaho. With one glassed over, fuzzy-looking eye, he was doing time for petty theft and homelessness. Woodchip John didn't have a hard convict's ethos. When he was out, he stole silver jewelry from touristy gift shops and sold the silver to be melted down and made into high-end jewelry.

When the fountain drink machine was broken and the two were working together in the kitchen, they mixed the Kool-Aid powder in two Igloo coolers—the other two were reserved for ice water. However, when Woodchip John mixed the drink packet, he mistakenly put a small amount of Kool-Aid powder in each cooler.

"It was diluted and tasted terrible," Dave said. "The people who wanted water were pissed because they got it mixed with Kool-Aid. The people who wanted Kool-Aid were pissed because they got watered down Kool-Aid."

When Kool-Aid was mixed in the coolers it left an unfortunate residue that would leave the water tasting like watered down Kool-Aid for the foreseeable future. People knew Dave and Woodchip John were responsible. Many people hassled Dave about the drink situation. Dave asked Woodchip John if he could do a better job mixing them, but he maintained a cavalier attitude. If they wanted it to be different, they could make it for themselves.

"I understand that in the hierarchy of table wipers, you've been a table wiper longer," Dave told Woodchip John. "So, you're the head table wiper, and I'm your assistant. But this Kool-Aid thing is a real problem."

Woodchip John became defiant.

Newly incarcerated, Dave then made one of the biggest mistakes during his entire time in prison.

He didn't realize that everyone in the prison's employ is a cop. Thinking she was a civilian subcontractor, Dave asked the woman overseeing kitchen workers if she could help mitigate the Kool-Aid situation. Dave thought it would be the perfect opportunity to ask her because she was alone in the kitchen with a highly regarded gang member, Country. Dave hoped that Country would vouch for Dave and confirm that he, in fact, did not rat on Woodchip John. Instead, Country's jaw dropped with disbelief.

"I'm looking at Country, and I'm all proud of myself because you're here to vouch that I didn't rat, and your guys are bitching about Kool-Aid more than anybody," Dave said. "So, all this is going to work out right. People are going to have the Kool-Aid they want. Everything is going to be smooth, and I'm going to be heralded as some kind of solver of problems. It didn't work that way at all."

Country immediately told his gang's shot-callers that Dave was a rat for throwing his coworker under the bus. Although Dave committed a significant faux pas, so did Country. The gang members were less worried about Dave ratting and more worried about Country being alone with a cop, which earned him a beating. When gang members are alone with cops, others suspect they were ratting or making deals with them.

"He's walking around with black eyes," Dave said. "He came and talked with me out on the yard, and basically told me that he thought I was a bitch. His feelings were hurt very badly because he had been beaten up."

Dave's rat reputation ultimately followed him to Sterling where both Dave and Country were transferred. Country told Dave's cellmate about his reputation. His cellmate thought it was idiotic, but would forgive him because he was new.

In the meantime, Woodchip John made a deal: Dave would make the Kool-Aid, clean it out afterward, and wipe down every table. Woodchip John would just hang around.

"To him, it became a matter of pride," Dave said.

For Dave this was a big lesson.

Being labeled as a snitch or a rat is one of the worst things that can happen to a person in prison. Snitching has big implications. Many people are serving time as a result of snitching. Coerced confessions and dirty deals from prosecutors make this a reality for many.

———

Rats and Snitches

Not all snitching is equal. *Rats* comprise those who snitch directly to officers. They are revered on the same level as chomos. *Dry snitching* happens when a person in prison doesn't overtly snitch, but rather talks to officers about a given situation.

If a corrections officer asks a prisoner where his cellmate is, it is against the inmate rules to divulge any information. There are only two acceptable answers to that question.

The first is: "I don't know."

The second, and more aggressive, is: "It is your job to know where inmates are, not mine. Why are you asking me to do your job for you?"

Giving any information about another inmate is considered "dry snitching" and is severely frowned upon.

When I heard about fiascos like the Kool-Aid one, my mind spiraled into dozens of other situations that could have led Dave into trouble. Dave told me more in one conversation about the hard days. For him, most of his days were good days. I was surprised he could describe any days spent in prison as *good*. However, to Dave, any day when his head hit the pillow without a confrontation was good.

People working in the kitchen could fasten food to their bodies with plastic wrap in the locker rooms. Prison uniforms, intentionally bought too large for the wearer, would hide food packages attached to the body. If successfully undertaken, people were able to smuggle food past the officers without detection. The locker rooms were only monitored by video cameras that were mounted on the ceiling, so it was a place of high activity and stress.

One day, a fight erupted between two men in the locker room, leaving one with a bloody, broken nose. When officers opened the door to allow people back into their living units, they noticed blood on the floor. No one was willing to answer their questions. After reviewing the security footage, the officers saw kitchen workers stealing food. All the workers in question were fired from the kitchen and other punishments were imposed upon them, including being placed in the hole. The workers viewed the man who bled on the floor as a snitch.

Dave explained that had the man who bled on the floor wiped up his own blood quickly, there would have been no incentive for the officers to review the security camera footage from that day in the locker room.

"So, his inaction was the catalyst that led to punishment for other offenders," Dave said. "Thus, he was admonished for snitching."

Another way one can get labelled a dry snitch is being caught with bartered items. If caught with another's belongings, both people are in trouble. Trouble is contingent on the nature of the relationships between the involved people.

"When dry snitching occurs between guys who are friends, there are usually no hard feelings because it is understood that a room shake-down is a surprise event and getting caught with another guy's property is just a piece of bad luck," Dave told me. "But, when dry snitching occurs between guys who are on less-than-friendly terms to begin with, dry snitching can lead to a severe fight."

Sterling Correctional Facility

The low side of Sterling

While Dave was at Sterling Correctional Facility, a medium-security prison, officers performed monthly shakedowns, usually on the first of the month. After the first rooms were searched, people would hide small-time contraband, like books and pornography. On the hard days, officers would perform random and retaliatory shakedowns. According to Dave, this was one way that cops could hold power over them.

Rusty

Rusty was Dave's cellmate. Rusty, now in his 60s, has been in prison since he was 16. He considers himself a hardcore convict and is highly respected among the influential prisoners. Dave's placement with such a convict was an educational experience.

During a shakedown, officers removed Dave from the room and strip-searched him. They ordered Dave to divulge information about Rusty. Dave responded by saying he didn't know anything about his business. Rusty was upset. Dave shouldn't have spoken a word to the cops. As a result, Dave felt he couldn't win in the great war between the prison system and the convict culture. The cops were able to exert power over his body by strip-searching him and he had inadvertently broken the rules of convict conduct.

Rusty in his natural habitat, sitting atop a Harley Davidson.

Dave is grateful that he never was raped or beaten up and that he never got into immense trouble with the cops. Not many people who have been incarcerated can say the same.

Dave had to be selfish in prison, while maintaining friendships with people who were fully indoctrinated by prison culture. According to the National Institute of Justice, almost 44 percent of people who are recently released from prison return before the end of their first year out. Dave combatted this revolving door mentality by focusing on self-improvement.

People who commit crimes aren't shown much forgiveness. When Dave was released from prison, he was unable to obtain a position at Home Depot or get an apartment, even in lower-income areas. Yet prison culture is just as unforgiving. Reputations are maintained for a lifetime.

"Nobody ever forgets anything about your reputation," Dave said. "There are so many aspects to the culture that are completely hypocritical."

Maybe because this is all they are shown from the world.

"People who are incarcerated are completely robbed of power," Dave said. "I had to stand and get counted at 6 o'clock. It didn't matter if I wanted to sleep in. I had to do exactly what they told me to do, most of the time."

Dave thinks convicts acting like authority figures is an effort to regain some semblance of power in their lives.

"They did it mostly through intimidation," Dave said.

Of course, the lack of power bothered Dave; but like a thunderstorm, he knew it would pass.

4

Prison Hustles

"Ask and it will be given to you; seek and you will find; knock and the door will be opened to you."
Matthew 7:7

Everything in prison can be a hustle. Nothing is done for free. Dave and I often met at the public library for our interviews. We always exceeded our allotted time in the study rooms. When we talked about Dave's first hustle in prison we had to move to the children's area of the library. In hushed tones we discussed times when he sold pictures of female celebrities to others in prison. It was the first hustle to earn Dave a prison living.

According to Dave, the most popular pictures were of Rihanna, Bo Derek, and Farrah Fawcett—for the older guys. Each photo ran for about one or two dollars, which was high by prison standards. Dave contracted out the work and tasks involved in such an endeavor. Tim reluctantly agreed to send the photos to Dave in prison. Guards, who searched all mail, didn't object to images of women, with the proviso that they were clothed in at least a thong or pasties.

"Basically, I'm sending him dollar bills," Tim said. "So, I'm spending my Saturday trying to load my thumb drive with these photographs, searching all this crazy stuff on my computer."

Tim told his partner at the time that if she got curious and went through his browser history that it was for Dave, not something weird.

"Tim was a good sport," Dave said.

Tim took specific requests all while being careful not to infringe on copyright laws. He then put photos on a thumb drive and downloaded them at Walgreens. As the pictures downloaded on a large screen, customers stared at him. He learned to send the photos in remotely but experienced the same problem with the Walgreen's employee who printed them out.

Luckily Tim didn't have to search for new pictures every time.

"Then I realized that the population in those areas turns over so quick that I just started sending the same pictures," Tim said. "So, my browser history was interesting."

Later in his sentence, Dave saw his original pictures pinned to bulletin boards and circulating around for profit—a weird circle of life moment.

———

Stores

Every prison has a commissary, which sells snacks and other items. At each prison there are several commissaries, segregated by race. Each store keeps commissary items and then sells them with interest to store patrons. Dave started a store with Rusty when the "white store's" boss got high and consumed all the merchandise. Dave collected the money and made the orders from the commissary. Rusty enforced payment and served as a security guard for the merchandise. Rusty had a sweet tooth, usually consuming a box of Little Debbies and a honey bun every night before bed, so running a store gave him incentive to have his sweets tax-free and housed in his cell.

Dave ordered about $100 worth of food items off the canteen list. If a customer had requests, they gave Dave money for two of the specific items. If customers got two packages of oatmeal cream pies from the store, they would have to order three from the canteen list and bring them back to the store. In less than a month Rusty and Dave went from having $100 worth of food to $225, minus what Rusty consumed, which was considerable. Eventually, he was put on a $30-dollar-per-week snack allowance. If customers were unwilling to pay, Rusty would mobilize the members in his gang. Once the word spread that their ability to collect was solid, almost all would pay.

"It was really such a sense of protection," Dave said. "As long as I didn't cross the line, everything was really, really easy."

Some lost their snacks on the poker table. If they were good inmates, Dave would sometimes extend their deadline by a week; he would keep the matter between him and the person in question, without Rusty's involvement. Dave walked a fine line of being a bitch or a ball buster. Any time new prisoners arrived, Dave would bring $10 worth of food to their cell. Eventually they racked up over $1,000 worth of merchandise. When the store supplies couldn't fit in their cell, Dave transferred them to other people's footlockers, offering a small salary for their service.

Once, Dave had spread out the food and his owe sheet on his bed when suddenly the fire alarm started going off—someone had either pulled it or had been smoking. During the evacuation to the yard, Dave looked up to see three cops pulling the blankets back in his room.

"The trick is to never say a word," Dave said. "I knew it from talking to the detective and talking my way into prison."

Rusty, always looking after himself, warned Dave that the

worst possible thing he could do was mention Rusty's name. Dave already knew not to mention names. The owe sheet was written in code so in case of an incident such as this, no one's name would be compromised.

When asked what the owe sheet was by the cops, Dave responded with short answers like, "it's a piece of paper." The cops did not have enough information to prove Dave and Rusty were running a store from their cell.

Fortunately for Dave, the cops had bigger things to worry about at a medium-level security prison, so no one looked too hard into the case. With people often overdosing and leaving on stretchers, the cops had to choose their battles.

One week prior to Dave's owe sheet confiscation, an inmate named 40, who used a wheelchair, was being housed in an A.D.A. compliant cell. He refused to live in the cell with a white cellmate. Cops forced him into the cell as he locked the wheels of his wheelchair. An alpha response was called as half a dozen cops arrived quickly. Refusing to comply with their orders, 40 got up from his chair and punched a female officer in the face twice, knocking her out.

"There was such an enormous hubbub around that," Dave told me. "Offender assault on staff doesn't happen very often. When it does happen, it's automatically the first priority."

Sex Work

Dave is commonly asked if he was raped in prison. He is grateful this was not his reality. He explained the climate to me. There were many guys in prison who didn't feel comfortable coming out as gay because they didn't want to be targeted. Openly gay guys often relied on having protectors. Those with protectors were called feezies. The protectors took ownership over feezies, feezies received protection. Feezies offered sex work in return for payment. The only instances of rape that Dave knew about occurred when sex workers would not receive compensation for their work. Sex work in prison seemed to pay well. Dave often observed that they ordered whatever they wanted on canteen order day.

"Once canteen day rolled around, you could see these guys carrying their whole bag of whatever they ordered into the room and dropping it off," Dave said. "They had as much of everything as they wanted."

Aside from their monetary stability, according to prison standards, gay inmates were treated with contempt. Many gangs stipulated that members couldn't eat with or enter a gay inmate's cell.

———

Chiropractic Work and Counsel

Many people performed jobs in prison that reflected their external professions. With prison mattresses and pillows that felt like cinder blocks, Dave became a popular chiropractor on the inside. Dave earned his prison nickname, Doc, from his medical work.

"My cell always became kind of a medical office," Dave said.

Charging far less than market value, Dave would instead sometimes charge stamps and food in return for chiropractic adjustments. He realized that some people became resentful if he charged money. Aside from the trades, Dave felt safer by giving this service.

"It put me in good standing with a lot of guys because they wanted to get adjusted and they knew that I wasn't over-charging or trying to exploit people, and they also knew I wasn't being a bitch and doing it for free," Dave said. "It worked out really well that way."

Prison bunks were about the approximate height for doing adjustments; Dave didn't need equipment.

Two weeks into his time at Burlington, an imposing guy, Lowry, came into Dave's "office." Standing about 6'2" and weighing about 275 pounds, Lowry had swastikas tattooed on his temples. He was one of the most physically imposing guys in the unit.

Lowry asked Dave his rate for an adjustment. Dave simply requested that Lowry didn't kill him. He became a regular patient, getting adjustments about once a week.

Dave said he saw more patients than the prison medical system. He helped people with significant problems, such as chronic migraines. Beyond seeing patients, Dave knew how to write reports for injuries that allowed quicker medical attention from prison staff. Dave told me that if a patient were having headaches, he might have to wait a month for a medical office visit. But, if Dave wrote that said patient was experiencing severe headaches accompanied by nausea and dizziness like no prior headache, he would get a visit within a day. That particular verbiage is related to headaches accompanying a stroke or vertebra-basilar artery incident, which is an emergency.

"I tried to use my knowledge and education to help other guys as often as possible," Dave said. "It was what I could contribute to the prisoner versus prison conflict that is omnipresent."

Dave remembers guys like Sean who used their prison knowledge to help him when he needed it for protection. Dave used his knowledge to pay that forward.

"I did a lot of advocating for guys when it came to their conflicts with the medical department," Dave said. "The true convicts respected that knowledge and the way I used it to fight against the system from the inside. The fake convicts resented anyone who had more knowledge than them."

As a chiropractor on the outside, a significant part of Dave's job was helping patients after auto accident-related injuries. Adept at writing reports, after his own bus accident, Dave knew he would be able to profit from his talents. Dave wrote his own medical reports delineating the injuries sustained in the bus accident. After seeing the prison doctors, he initiated a lawsuit against the private prison corporation too.

After his stay in the hole in Colorado Springs following the bus accident, Dave visited the doctor at Burlington Prison. He complained of shoulder, neck, and hand pain, all on his left side. The prison physician's assistant conducted a foot exam because they ran out of the documents pertaining to neck exams.

"That was the moment I decided to sue CCA. When they are doing exams based upon which forms they have handy as opposed to what the patient's complaint is," Dave said.

It was easier to hire a lawyer for his lawsuit against the food distribution company because auto accident suits are common. A settlement with the food distribution company ended in Dave receiving $150,000, which he received several years later. Lawsuits against private prison companies fall under civil rights law, which is less common. Dave sued the private prison company on the grounds of deliberate indifference, meaning the authorities were aware of a serious problem, but made no effort to resolve the matter. Dave started his studies at the law library in the prison and looked for precedents.

A couple months into our project, Dave texted me that he lost the lawsuit against the prison company. His lawyer was remiss in hiring an expert witness to testify to Dave's injuries. Both assumed that Dave would qualify as an expert witness due to his profession. Dave was grateful that he received some settlement money to start his life upon release.

While doing research for his cases, he realized he had an

affinity for law work. Other inmates began asking him for assistance with their cases. Dave helped appeal cases that were illegal in their wording. He also helped appeal many erroneously worded concurrent or consecutive sentences. If a guilty verdict is entered for two different offenses or more, but all arise from one criminal event, the sentences must be served concurrently in Colorado. Many judges make a myriad of mistakes when writing sentences, which results in more prison time.

Dave also appealed write-ups people received as punishments in prison. Dave was paid well by prison standards, sometimes receiving 50 stamps or chocolate cakes. For inmates who were illiterate, he read court documents aloud along with letters from friends and family.

"Having the reputation of being the guy who reduces sentences really endeared me to convicts and inmates and NACs and everybody," Dave said. "Everybody likes someone who is stealing time back from the police."

Dave was once written up for receiving ten tokens. The giver of the tokens wanted to express personal appreciation for Dave, not considering that there would be video evidence of the exchange. Before the footage was reviewed, Dave changed into gym clothes before cops patted him down. Dave noted that during the hearing, the cops failed to adhere to the correct procedures. In particular, they didn't provide the evidence of the tokens. Dave submitted a written appeal to the warden. He decided to have a new hearing. Even though there was evidence present at the new hearing, Dave argued that the double jeopardy law protected him. New evidence couldn't deem him guilty. Dave was found not guilty and the officers were ordered to return the illicitly obtained tokens.

Cheekily, Dave asked the officer to deliver the tokens to his cell.

Dave then served as an inmate representative for recipients

of disciplinary write-ups. These trials were set up like court-rooms, with Dave serving as the public defender for inmates. In general, inmates were found guilty because cops avoided under-mining fellow cops. Dave, being well-aware of these norms, relied on failure to adhere to protocol to win trials. Dave asked the police many questions and later wrote an appeal to the warden. The appeal addressed the cops' failure to adhere to trial protocols.

This allowed Dave to win about half of his trials.

"It's all about flipping the script," Dave said. "I always tried to do that in my mind. Instead of feeling like I was being preyed upon, I could feel like the predator against the system."

These actions allowed Dave to try and reclaim some author-ity. He had legal outlets to do so.

Dave still works with the law. He started his own consulting business, Suro Consulting. He serves as a broker of sorts, connecting incarcerated people looking to sue for medical malpractice with civil rights lawyers. Dave also has connections with friends on the inside like Sean, who reach out to those interested in legal services on the inside. Dave then sifts out cases that won't stand up in court.

At the time of writing, Dave is currently working with a man who had an untreated case of Methicillin-resistant Staphylo-coccus aureus that resulted in amputation of his leg.

Dave is also working with a man who had an untreated disease which led to detached retinas in both eyes. He is now blind.

Dave works with a man who has hydrocephalus, with an Arnold Chiari malformation. His brain swelling is pushing his brain into his neck vis-a-vis the little hole in the base of his skull. The man is in the tragic and rapid process of becoming a quadriplegic.

Why?

He is not receiving treatments that would slow down this process.

Sometimes Dave receives delusional calls. Recently, he received a letter from a man in San Carlos Prison in Pueblo, Colorado. San Carlos is a mental facility that specializes in rehabilitating male inmates who suffer from mental health problems. He believes that if he cuts himself enough, the prison will go bankrupt from paying for his stitches and release all inmates. Dave often tells me he speaks three languages: medical, convict, and lawyer.

"Given my set of circumstances, which are very unusual, the only way this business plan could work is if I were a doctor who became an inmate who studied law for five years in there and had Rusty as a cellmate because he taught me how to speak convict," Dave said.

While Dave was in the nascent stages of establishing his consulting business, he also started his own tree work company. I spoke with one of his tree work clients, Matt Fowls. They became friends after Dave discovered Matt is a small business and startups attorney.

"We got several estimates because we like to shop around for a deal, my wife and I," Matt told me while we met at his office. "Dave was not even close to the cheapest. He was the nicest. He was definitely the person who was present for the conversation. Very much attentive to our concerns. You get good energy from people sometimes and he is one of those people."

Matt has seen various types of intermediary work like real estate brokers, but has never seen brokers who work with lawyers and people in prison.

"I have never seen anything close to resembling what he's trying to do," Matt said. "I think it's great. I think he's smart enough. I think he's well equipped enough. I think he's got all the right things going for him to succeed."

Matt's younger brother inspired him to go to law school. His brother has severe mental health issues. Matt attended a criminal defense clinic at Denver University.

"It seems like with this population of folks, we find places to store them, and prison is one of those places," Matt said.

Matt and I talked about the problems with the criminal justice system in the United States. "These labels that we put people into, it's something that's practical to categorize things, but they cannot be overused and misused like they are in our society," Matt said. "We put people in boxes and never let them out."

Convict Mentality

"Come to me, all you who are weary and burdened, and I will give you rest. Take my yoke upon you and learn from me, for I am gentle and humble in heart, and you will find rest for your souls. For my yoke is easy and my burden is light."
    Matthew 11:28

I spent a large portion of this project figuring out what separates those who identify as convicts from those who do not. There are no explicit definitions. Some who once identified as convicts no longer do so; some are the reverse. Convicts are often defined by their long sentences in prison and their rejection of society's laws. They see life as one lengthy fight against the legal and prison systems.

With a shorter sentence and intentions to follow civilian rules, Dave was never a convict.

Rusty is.

"He's unrepentant," Dave said. "But that's one of the things I love about him. He's just this absolute pure form of truth. I have to respect his honesty. I learned a lot from him, and I'm better for the experience of living with him."

Rusty, who was described to me by many as a cranky, old, red-bearded Santa Claus looking dude, never had a cellmate like Dave.

"I first met him when he came to Sterling and became my cellie," Rusty wrote to me in a letter. "I looked out on the yard and saw some tall-ass dude heading toward my cell block, and since I had an empty bed in my cell, I figured he was probably headed there. Whether I was going to let him stay or not was another story. I could tell he was a fish."

Rusty describes himself as old school.

"I want to know where you came from," Rusty said, "what you are in for and what you are about. Who you ride with, etc., and that means check your paperwork, check your background and verify anything you tell me. Please excuse me for sounding rude or bullying or anything like that. Prison is a totally different world, ya know? And even though we were in a medium security yard at the time, that's not where I started. I've done time in bike clubs, so I suppose I come off a little non-friendly."

When Dave moved into Rusty's cell, Rusty wouldn't talk to him until his Hell's Angels lawyers completed their background check. The lawyers look out for falsified paperwork. Those with unpopular crimes can falsify their paperwork to avoid conflict. The word on the yard was that Dave was questionable, but not terrible like a rat, chomo, or sex offender, but questionable. If Dave would have fallen into the former category, Rusty would have given him the ultimatum of leaving the cell or fighting him to the death.

"A lot of times, it depends on who you live with as to how you are gonna be treated," Rusty said. "The fact that he was my cellie would give him a little more acceptance initially. Everyone that matters would automatically assume that I've done my homework and checked his paperwork and character out. The fact that he's living with me means I'm vouching for him to a certain extent."

Rusty started serving time in solitary confinement and high security prisons, where he didn't see many offenders like Dave. Rusty hoped that Dave had an easier time because of him.

"We gave each other space," Rusty said. "Try to be on different schedules. We had some fun times, comparing lifestyles and shit like that. We didn't have a whole lot in common I suppose, but that made it funny sometimes."

Rusty also benefited from knowing Dave.

"He was probably the first one I liked or trusted," Rusty said. "I've done a lot of years in solitary, so I haven't had a whole lot of cellies, but by the time I met Dave I had made it to a lower custody yard and they aren't so worried about who they move in with you, as long as you are white and not a sex offender, they'll move you in together and let nature take its course, I guess. I think I was the only one labeled as S.T.G. on our floors at the time, so they didn't have a whole lot of options. They have to fill beds, ya know? And I suppose they knew if I didn't want him there, he wouldn't be staying. I have kicked out several cellies or not even let them move in period, over the years. But at that point I hadn't had a lot of cellies."

It was somewhat odd for the prison to house a convict with a history of gang involvement with a newly incarcerated person in the same cell. Officers stopped Dave on the yard to warn him. However, it would have been unacceptable for Dave to say he didn't want to live with Rusty. That answer would label him a rat indefinitely.

One of the first things Rusty told Dave was that he believed in three things: money, power and violence.

"It's funny because he's really such a sweetheart, but he doesn't really put on a false front because he was a Hell's Angel for decades," Dave said. "I don't think he's ever followed a law on purpose in his entire life. He's a true outlaw motorcycle guy."

Dave knew that Rusty was the cell boss. He was neither rude nor deferential. When he needed the cell for a couple of hours, there was no discussion. Dave would leave. Dave worked around Rusty's schedule. Dave didn't ask questions about why Rusty needed the cell.

"When we were in the cell together in Sterling, Rusty used to talk about how he's getting really old, and he didn't know how to do anything other than be a criminal," Dave said. "He would always want to talk about how he wanted to die in one last big shootout and take a couple of cops with him."

When Rusty heard about Dave's plans for me to write the book, he had just finished reading *The Animal Factory*—a book about two men who met in San Quentin prison.

"I think it's funny that I just finished reading that book, and then I get a letter from you saying that you are writing a book," Rusty wrote to Dave. "Coincidence, huh?"

Dave put money on Rusty's prison account. Rusty was grateful because he wasn't doing too well on his most recent prison sentence.

Rusty was released to a halfway house in July 2017. He walked out of the house two months later and spent his days indulging in motel stays and bike rides. Later he got a couple of hot urinalysis tests.

"All in all, I ran amok for about six months and ended up in a high-speed chase (my third one) in a car coming down the mountain from Georgetown one night," Rusty wrote to Dave.

He was sent back to prison to finish his sentence.

"I feel real positive about the future," Rusty wrote in his letter to Dave. "I have total faith in completing this parole and putting this shit behind me. I'm old ya know? I've slowed down. I'm done with all this partying and shit. I've done it all ya know. I'm ready for the slow lane. I'm actually looking forward to it. I'll always have a couple bikes. I plan to ride as long as I can, of course, but I'm officially retired from the club. I'm in good standing, which means a lot, of course. And even though I've sacrificed a lot over the years, I'm content. I love them, but I'm out. I'm looking forward to riding with my son one day. I have a bunch of grandkids I've never seen, but I will one day. My uncle passed away, but my dad is still kicking, barely, but he's still around. I hope to see him once more before he passes."

Rusty and I began epistolary correspondences of our own. He told me about his life. He wrote that his life was probably much different than Dave's. Rusty grew up in New York with his mother. He ran with smaller street gangs and started doing drugs at age 13. At 14, he ran away to Florida where he sold mopeds to tourists and lived off stolen grocery store food and drug dealing. When he returned to New York, he was arrested for stealing a car. The judge gave him a deal: join the army or stay in jail.

Rusty was in the Army from 1973 through 1975. During these years, he smuggled drugs from Mexico and built motorcycles. He was caught several times at the border, but it wasn't a big deal at the time, Rusty told me. At age 20, recently released from the Army, Rusty began running around with bike clubs. His first shoot-out with another club resulted in losing a kidney, two ribs, and half of his stomach. He served jail time. By 1982, Rusty served prison time in New York for assault, leaving behind his two-year-old son, Harley. Rusty told me he's been in street gangs, motorcycle clubs, and prisons his entire adult life.

"I've been shot three times and done about 25 years in prison," Rusty said. "I have long hair, long beard, and tattoos covering most of my body. Dave is clean cut, educated, and probably has no tattoos. Also never been to prison before or been through any of the things I've been through, so that's why we come from different worlds."

Dave doesn't have tattoos.

"I've changed more toward his kind of life than he has toward mine—despite the fact that he went to prison," Rusty said. "He's still a citizen I'm sure—just a little more enlightened one I bet."

Rusty thinks that labels can have a major impact on people in prison. But it depends on who assigns the label: the prison or the inmates. For him, it's hard to learn lessons from an institution that insists on labeling people—labels that might not be truly defining of a person.

"What lessons can you learn in here that would matter on the outside?" Rusty asked in his letter to me. "Hopefully you already know those lessons: common respect, don't underestimate anyone. I'm sure after living around so many shady people, you'd be a little more suspicious. I'm sure you leave these places a little more jaded than you came in, and a little less trusting. I'll bet that I'm talking more about authority figures than I am about inmates."

Rusty was approved by the parole board for release in April 2020. He took classes and received no write-ups for a year. Pressured by the COVID-19 pandemic and its threat to prison populations, Rusty's parole board agreed to release him. Dave agreed to pick Rusty up from the prison on his release date. Rusty hopes that he can someday move back to New York to be with his father and daughter. Dave thinks this is the best course of action for Rusty. Dave thinks that most of Rusty's connections in Colorado are pipelines to illegal activity.

———

True Convicts

I don't like labels. Putting together this book has reinforced this even more. In some cases, however, labels fit very well.

In Dave's opinion, Kodiak is a true convict. The 70-year-old from Alaska first went to prison for killing several people.

"Kodiak just killed people," Dave said. "That's just what he did."

Shortly after his release, he moved to California and killed someone after an argument. After his release in California, he moved to Colorado and killed again. Now he knows he will spend the remainder of his life in prison.

"He was a really cool guy," Dave said. "In prison he was the most mild-mannered guy."

When they played Scrabble, Dave became comfortable enough to ask why Kodiak killed so many.

He told Dave that it was his way of solving arguments.

"And I thought to myself, don't argue with Kodiak because it doesn't go well," Dave said. "But in my opinion, he was a true convict because he didn't live within the rules of society, obviously."

Kodiak was frail when Dave knew him, but he never walked around with the gait of a tough man. He didn't have to. The idealist in me wants to set everyone serving time in prison free, but what would this look like for the Kodiaks of the world?

———

Spooky

I met Spooky at a hipster cafe called Novo. Starbucks, he said, would have worked just as well. He seemed uncomfortable to be in the trendy joint.

Dave thought he earned his nickname because of the spider tattoo on his head. Spooky told me that he would always bet on Dave when he played Scrabble. He would also come to him if he was hurt or wanted to play a game of poker.

"He was always there helping people, fixing people, clowning, sitting there and telling funny stories, playing cards, talking about people that came in and out, that got out for a week or two and screwed up their life and got even more time," Spooky said.

Spooky told me he saw Dave as a citizen who didn't belong in prison. Some thought it was funny they hung out together considering their differences.

"People look at me and they see the people I kick it with and they kinda trip, but Dave was like one of the ones I introduced to all of my people because of his special skills," Spooky said.

A recurring notion expressed by many of my interviewees was that all prison relationships should be mutually beneficial.

"The way I know him is that anytime I needed something he would help out," Spooky told me. "In a situation when you're in prison, you pretty much want to know the right people and be cool with them people."

Dave benefitted from knowing Spooky. He could help out if chaos ensued. Dave could drop Spooky's name to obtain security for the store he ran or if he got into trouble. Spooky also had enough clout with his gang affiliation, along with the amount of time he served. With a past in hard drugs, Spooky used to be a shot-caller for a gang. He spent many years in solitary on the high security sides of prisons. Gang members are often housed in these sides of prisons. There he spent a lot of time soul searching and reading the Bible, he told me. A big reason he gave up the lifestyle was for his mother, who is devoutly religious. Spooky is honored that she put her sons' names on the Jerusalem Wall.

"Me and my brothers have done the most, none of us have been really hurt," Spooky said. "We're all still alive. It's because of my mom's prayers."

After significant rumination, Spooky concluded he needed to step back from the gang and spend time with his mother and children. Spooky prayed for a way out. As this book has made clear, renouncing gang affiliation all too frequently ends in violence. Subsequently, a member of the gang asked him to quietly step down because he would be moving living units. Spooky is grateful for this peaceful end to his period as a gang member.

Spooky on his way to work post-release.

Spooky has been out of prison for about a year and a half. As a former meth abuser, he realizes that his message can reach many who struggle. He remains grateful for the small things.

"Thank God I have all my teeth," Spooky said. "I have an appreciation for God because I could be totally messed up."

Now, Spooky worries about other family members who are addicts and navigating life outside of prison. Despite his many car chases with police in the past, Spooky got his first driver's license just this year.

"It is hard to be good, let me tell you—trying to go to work and pay all them bills," Spooky said. "Something's gotta give. That's why I don't go to the streets. I see the same people and they're doing the exact same thing, never change. They're just missing teeth, looking older. It's a bad thing."

Dave spent time with Spooky in a low-security facility. Both were to be released soon. Dave saw Spooky interact with his family. He threw the ball back and forth with his nephew.

"He's uncle Tommy at that point," Dave said. "To see people shifting gears and interacting with their family was really cool."

———

Crisp

I met Crisp at Texas Roadhouse, where he's a corporate trainer. We met during his break. Despite stretches of prison time, his manager always lets him resume his duties at the restaurant. I can see why. He immediately put me at ease, maintaining a big grin as we talked over glasses of sweet tea. Crisp is passionate about music, with a particular affinity for speed metal. He is a singer, songwriter and producer. Prison supported his music career. Crisp had access to instruments, recording studios, an audience, and hours of free time to practice.

"The bands that I've played with in prison are the best bands I've played with in my life," Crisp said. "The music that we wrote and played in there is stuff you would hear on the radio."

Dave attended Crisp's concerts. Crisp told me that even the

cops would enjoy his music. His band liked to cover softer songs by artists like Taylor Swift, to the cops' pleasant surprise.

Crisp has been in and out of prison for the last 16 years. Now in his early 50s, Crisp has learned how to stay out and remain focused. He was addicted to meth and to having children—he has six. One prison sentence was caused by him slinging a bag of meth over a prison wall while on parole. Crisp now reaches out to children, cautioning them against falling into his old lifestyle.

Dave reminded Crisp of external life.

"I'm just a normal person who had a drug problem," Crisp said. "Spending time with him was refreshing, like spending time on the outside."

Crisp said Dave would help him stay focused on the positive facets of life. He also said Dave had a positive influence on many and was a good judge of character. Dave's persistence, Crisp said, helped him foster friendships in prison.

"For some people, prison is really easy," Crisp said. "For him to make it easy, his advantage was how smart he is, his size, and just knowing how to stay out of bullshit."

Crisp looking motivated at the gym after his release.

However, Crisp observed that some perceived Dave's knowledge as belittlement. As an educated white man, perhaps for the first time in his life, Dave learned the practice of not talking. Even if he knew something was factually incorrect, he learned the value of not correcting others. Dave could often change the subject to the weather or sports when conversations got heated. As a Tampa Bay Buccaneers football fan, he was able to bet on and brag about his team because they often lost. This served as a way to diffuse tense conversations.

"His education enabled him to check them every once and a

while when they would try to bully some of the other inmates, he would kinda go to bat for them," Crisp said.

Now Crisp is writing a book with his family about what to do when your children commit crimes. Crisp's mother and stepfather had little direct exposure to crime before their son began committing them.

———

Brain

I met with Brain at a local cafe in my hometown. He earned his nickname because his bald head resembles a brain. Dave told me to check out the side of his head when we met, so I could really see the brain shape. I was too embarrassed.

Brain was recently released from a 14-year prison sentence for his involvement in a non-lethal shoot out with a police officer. He told me he was addicted to drugs at the time of the shootout. His crime earned him respect from convicts. To them, shooting a cop is the best crime one can commit. His crime earned him the opposite treatment from cops. His parole officer still refuses to make eye contact with him.

"He had a much tighter connection with the hardcore

convicts than I did," Dave said. "He could go to any of them and ask for anything because he shot a cop."

Dave first met Brain at Sterling when he walked up with a poodle on a leash. Brain trained dogs for a dog program at the prison. The program used people in prison to train seven-week-old puppies into obedient dogs for owners or for law enforcement.

"He was such a devoted and loving dog trainer," Dave told me.

Brain demonstrating perfect dog handling technique.

When we met, Brain told me a great deal about dog training. He is especially passionate about the use of proper proto-cols in training dogs.

"Spending time in prison sucks, but spending time in prison with a dog is a little better," Brain said.

Brain is also passionate about his sobriety. In prison, he was outspoken about separating himself from people doing drugs. Dave describes Brain as extremely thoughtful. He often got up at 4 a.m. to write letters to loved ones without the influence of even a cup of coffee.

Brain and I had a long conversation. He explained many things to me about the prison system as someone who spent significant time incarcerated.

"Prison is just a negative place where it's all on you to determine the outcome," Brain told me. "It's on us as inmates or people to take what you want out of it into your hands. There were classes and there were things to improve yourself and there were also vices."

Because Brain was both experienced and thoughtful, he looked out for Dave, who could be naive. Hanging out with

Dave made Brain feel like a park ranger, instructing Dave of the looming dangers.

"I was so naive," Dave said. "I didn't understand."

Fellow inmates would be snorting Wellbutrin or meth lines from their desk, and Dave walked into the room as if he were visiting a neighbor. Brain knew this was a bad situation. If a cop entered the room later that day, Dave would have been suspected of snitching because he had seen the illicit activities.

"It was important to pretend I had blinders on, but I'm curious and outgoing and friendly by nature," Dave said. "Those are characteristics that just don't play well in prison."

Brain knew the dangers of living in a prison with 600 other men on his yard. He was also worried about Rusty's high standing among convicts and its implications, given Dave was his cellmate.

"He wasn't aware of the potential around him, which isn't a bad thing, but it could be a bad thing," Brain said. "Dave sticks out like a sore thumb, both in physical stature and his mind. So, he draws attention wherever he goes. It's not easy to blend in."

Most people I interviewed thought Dave stood out while in prison—not only because of his physical size. This may have led him into trouble, but for most, he reminded them of the external world.

"He was always a breath of fresh air for me in prison because he wasn't involved in all that stuff," Brain said. "When I went to talk to him it was about biking and going for a hike or his dog or his college days. He has some pretty silly stories. He always had positive input in there."

After we spoke about Dave, I asked Brain about his insights on prison culture and gang involvement. Dave certainly had considerable perspective on the culture, but it was valuable for me to talk with Brain. He had many years to reflect on it.

"Prison is like elementary school with grown men," Brain said. "It's horrible."

Before I met Brain, I was undecided on if I would include gang names in the book. Brain personally suggested that I avoid validating them by including their true names. Savvy to the nature of the prison gangs he spent time with, Dave divulged a lot of information about them. Although personally fascinated by gang culture, I decided to use little specifics about gangs in this book. Dave and many of the interviewees of the book warned of the danger of prison gang affiliation. Rather than attest to Dave's knowledge of gang inner-workings, I mostly avoided that subject for the safety of those involved in the book

"It's done out of fear of the unknown or not being able to stop something for themselves," Brain said about people joining prison gangs. "I think that some of those guys genuinely really are racist and they are teaching that hate and separatism to new guys."

He watched as white supremacist gang members uttered racist remarks to prisoners of color and looked around for validation.

"It's not just the hate, but the need to belong with someone for the flawed idea of feeling that hate and anger for another person just because they exist is going to end you back in prison because it's not going to stop with that person, you're going to start applying that to other people," Brain said.

Brain reflected on the consequences of that attitude.

"You're not going to seek to understand what it is that is good about that person," Brain continued. "And that difference is what makes people good, and it's going to make people go back to prison and do drugs and drink and continue to inflict harm on themselves and others."

Brain remained unaffiliated from gangs for his 14-year sentence, which was not an easy task. He was labelled a non-affiliated Caucasian, or what he likes to call "not a conflict."

"When I got to prison, I was scared, and I wanted to belong," Brain said.

Originally having a 38-year sentence, Brain's first cellmate was heavily involved in a California gang. He advised Brain to wait five years before getting any tattoos or joining any gangs.

"He altered the course of my life and my prison sentence," Brain said.

In particular, he encouraged personal betterment, namely by pushing Brain to learn to read and write. At first, Brain's motives did not constitute self-improvement by societal standards.

"I remember telling myself that I was going to be more dangerous when I left than when I went in," Brain told me.

But Brain's involvement in the dog program was the "-tipping point mentally," he said. "I stopped being selfish and gained some responsibility and started to be a decent human being."

Brain is a success story when it comes to people who serve long sentences in prison.

"The system's broken," Brain said. "There's no easy answer. There is no answer. It's a societal thing. The way we are raised and the way we are taught to think in this country is what the problem is. That's why there are so many people in prison in the United States and not in other parts of the world."

As a recovering addict, he recognizes that self-defeat and victimization leads to a pattern of further incarceration.

"There are a lot of really good guys in there, they just choose to not get up," Brain said. "They got knocked down, but they never get back up."

Brain is figuring out how to live in a world that is the antithesis of prison. He belongs to a group of recently released people who work out together. Although it was initially awkward to see them, they've become quite close, he told me.

———

Hobbies Behind the Wall

Before this project, I never considered incarcerated people's hobbies.

Dave spent a great deal of time playing games like chess, Scrabble, and bridge. Dave spent about an hour a day studying the Scrabble dictionary. Of course, nothing in prison is done without a price.

"Everyone was trying to make a little bit of money because it felt normal to make money," Dave said. "Everyone is trying to make a dollar—like literally, a dollar."

Beyond playing games, people in prison made and sold merchandise.

Sasse

Sasse was in prison for burning down his house. He wasn't a convict. He struggled with alcoholism and bipolar disorder. During his divorce with his wife, he got drunk and planned to kill himself in a fire he set to his former wife's house. He succeeded in burning down the house, but failed in taking his own life. Though the children were not home when he set the fire, Sasse received a child endangerment charge because of the emotional harm inflicted on his children from losing their home.

Anyone with a child endangerment charge is automatically looked at with suspicion in prison. Prosecutors often make deals with sex offenders of children by lowering their charge to child endangerment in return for a speedy plea bargain. Most avoided Sasse because of this questionable charge. Dave knew the full story and vouched for Sasse.

"I felt really bad for him because child endangerment is a crime that is looked at differently," Dave said. "He was treated pretty poorly."

Sasse post-release

Sasse kept to himself. He spent his time crocheting. He sold cozies, scarves, blankets, and lingerie for the gay inmates. Dave laughs remembering the time when a tornado hit the prison yarn factory. When the prison broadcasted the news, Dave thought it was the cops messing with them.

Tornados aside, the yarn factory got a surprising amount of use. Some inmates crocheted stuffed animals or did commissioned drawings. Others collected and cut strips of chip and snack bags and wove colorful baskets.

"Some of the art was just absolutely beautiful," Dave said. "It just blew my mind how talented some of these guys were."

Cory, who met Dave in prison, told me that incarcerated artists produced some of the best work he's ever seen.

The darkness of their situations, along with free time, often translates to impressive art.

"Some didn't even know they could draw, and they have this whole fucked up story that comes along with them," Cory said.

"There's a lot of pain in prison, a lot of fucked up family lives, a lot of people having to live with their own consciences. There's a lot of stuff there that creates growth."

Working out was another hobby for many. All three prisons offered intramural sports, which provided an interesting dynamic, namely because the teams required a referee—a role akin to a police officer. The referees were often beaten. Dave never participated because of the potential conflicts, but he thoroughly enjoyed watching.

"There was always an argument," Dave said. "I don't think I've ever laughed as hard in my life as I did watching prison intramural softball."

Cooking was another common hobby. People would order ingredients from the canteen list. They made batches of 50 burritos and sold them cell to cell.

Some were trying to be the next rap star.

Dave worked with Dupriest in the kitchen. He constantly mocked Dupriest's depressing poetry. Dave chalked it up to Dupriest's upbringing in a cult, which affected his sociability.

Some would just sit and channel surf on T.V. for years.

"For some reason, the 'Home and Garden Network' was very popular," Dave said. "We don't have homes and we don't have gardens, but people loved it."

Dave watched Trump's 2016 election on a T.V. obtained from the prison black market. It was confiscated a month later.

"Trump was just so entertaining," Dave said. "He would get on there and start talking his crazy stuff and it just got everyone really fired up."

———

Rebels with a Cause

Unlike others with long sentences, Dave could separate himself from the convict mentality. He wasn't interested in extending his relatively short sentence by participating in convict behavior.

"As soon as somebody has a life sentence, that inhibition is gone," Dave said.

For someone incarcerated for life, there was little preventing him from committing crimes. If he decided to stab a child molester, the worst punishment he could receive in Colorado is a year spent in solitary, due to ACA guidelines.

Prison Day Room

Dave sometimes saw people doing heroin. He had to pinch himself because of the surrealness of the situation. Dave didn't avoid convict behavior all together, rather, he walked a fine line of helping the convicts when it wouldn't negatively affect his sentence. Dave helped by acting as a lookout or keeping tech. Dave sat in the day room near the C.O.'s office. When the officer got up to walk through the hallways, Dave would go ahead of the officer and give warning knocks on doors.

"I was helping the convicts in that way, which was a beneficial service, so they treated me well, but knew I wasn't really one of them, which frankly was a great place to be for me," Dave said. "Don't ask questions, mind my own business, and always keep a lookout in case the police are heading to the room for any reason, which happened quite a bit."

This is referred to as *keeping tech*. Dave didn't have to ask Rusty questions; he would simply alert him when cops were in the vicinity.

"The convict mentality is to basically always be fighting against the prison, and to accept you're a prisoner and define yourself as a prisoner," Dave said. "Convicts went one of two ways: they either became the nicest people you could imagine, or they became the most deplorable people you could imagine. They didn't ever seem to have any middle of the road."

Some lifers became very devoted to religion. Other convicts would do the same with learning the legal system in order to help other guys. They knew they had the rest of their life to work on an appeal, so they were trying to write the perfect one.

"They would essentially go insane with it because, deep down, I think they knew they had no chance of winning an appeal, but they were still trying," Dave said.

Some would appeal all the way to the Supreme Court.

Many convicts were filled with remorse and didn't identify with their crime all that much anymore, Dave explained. They had a certain level of detachment to the life they once led.

Dave also observed many convicts living life on the installment plan. This was a life of coming in and out of prison.

"What they wanted to do was see how much they could exploit other people, and how high they could get while they were in prison," Dave said. "They knew once they got out that they were going to come back. They were kinda more comfortable in the prison system because generally those were the guys who were joining gangs, and they enjoyed that wolf pack mentality. They were the most dangerous people."

As Dave explained this to me, I thought about the many ways that the prison system is remiss in its duty to rehabilitate. It teaches people a whole set of skills that will literally continue to help them fail following their release.

"Then, you'd get guys who had a three-year sentence, but they were trying to identify as convicts," Dave said. "They were just overplaying the whole thing. Like walking around scowling at everybody, trying to act real tough. It was weird because they were sort of playing a role that they haven't really earned the right to play because, jeez, they had a shorter sentence than me, they're going to be out in a year, but they're trying to identify as a lifer."

Dave doesn't understand those types of 'fake' convict's rationale. He said he generally didn't interact with them, noting that problems were all too likely to transpire.

"More often than not, their life on the streets was just so terrible that life was easier for them inside," Dave said.

Dave assumed a convict's mindset at times. Such was the dilemma: he strove to keep his mind free and engaged in external activities, but he also had to be involved in the prison culture sufficiently to maintain a good reputation.

"It turns out that convicts respect appropriate convict behavior, regardless of race," Dave said. "It is a complex dynamic. It's kind of like the codes of chivalry where knights from opposing armies way-back-when would follow the unspoken, archaic rules of fighting one another. For instance, a knight on horseback would never continue to fight a knight who had been dismounted from his horse. The dismounting was a victory in-and-of itself."

Dave remembers an incident involving his friend Thirsty. Thirsty was quietly arguing with two gang shot-callers at the bleachers on the yard. While walking laps around the track, Dave overheard Thirsty mention the shot-callers disrespecting him. Dave didn't know what to do. Standing next to Thirsty would threaten the shot-callers while simultaneously insinuating that Thirsty was too weak to take care of himself. It also implied that Dave was ear-hustling their conversation. If he kept walking and a fight ensued, the action would be perceived as abandoning a friend. Dave then decided to walk about fifteen feet more before turning to face Thirsty. He established quick eye contact so Thirsty knew Dave stopped on his behalf and stood silently, keeping the three of them in his peripheral vision. To stop and look directly at them would have been bad, even a little worse than ear-hustling. Thirsty knew he had a two-on-two situation if a fight broke out and knew Dave would be able to surprise the shot-callers. This would get them off Thirsty for the couple seconds needed for members of Thirsty's gang to intervene. Thankfully, a scuffle didn't ensue. Thirsty commended Dave on doing the right thing.

"The strange thing to me was that I actually was prepared to fight—a thought in the convict mentality," Dave said. "I wasn't hoping for a fight, at all, so I wasn't all-the-way convict at that moment, but it felt foreign to me and like home to me at the same time. Thinking back on it, it's strange to me how an act as subtle as stopping to let a guy know he wasn't alone could have such a complex chain of thoughts behind it. And, that such a subtle act still has such a profound impact on my memory. Nothing is more important than loyalty in a situation like that."

I wonder if Dave was ever prepared to defend a friend during a fist fight during his days as a chiropractor.

The Man Who Walks With Purpose

"And so I tell you, every kind of sin and slander can be forgiven, but blasphemy against the Spirit will not be forgiven."
Matthew 12:31

Chase

Dave met Chase at Delta, the final prison at which both served time. It was the lowest level of security, a level one, without even an electric kill fence. They became cellmates, having already become friends at the gym.

"I never got tired of his stories. We were in a 10-by-10 room a lot of hours together for over a year, and the whole time I was just entertained," Dave said.

Chase has been in prison nearly all his adult life, more than 30 years. Chase started doing his time when he was young. Back in the '80s and '90s, prison culture was considerably different. Chase was first sentenced to juvenile prison for breaking and entering when he was 16. Now he's in his early 50s.

Since he's been out of prison, Chase posts avidly on TikTok. He hopes to be a media influencer like the Kardashian family.

"He's over there reading People magazine because he thought being up to date on pop culture would be a great way for him to meet women when he gets out of prison," Dave laughed. "He studied it like it was his job."

Now, Chase aims to be featured in such entertainment magazines. I wonder if Chase hopes this book will bring him fame.

"He's a publicity hound, so anything that will get his name out there," Dave said. "He really thinks he's going to become an influencer and become a multi-millionaire."

Chase is extremely proud of his physique. Dave laughed, remembering how when new men were bused into the prison, Chase wore his t-shirt, which was two sizes too small, to show off his muscles.

Dave's height was also off-putting to Chase at first.

"Being tall did freak Chase out a bit," Dave said. "Chase is a true alpha male. So, at first my height intimidated him just a little bit, and then he realized I was just a big softy."

Chase came up with one of Dave's nicknames, "The Man Who Walks with Purpose." Dave walked Delta's perimeter as close to the fence as he could get, a little more than three fourths of a mile.

He usually walked about eight laps in two hours.

"I had a stopwatch, so I became borderline obsessive about timing myself to see how fast I could walk a lap," Dave told me. "Other people are strolling around on the yard acting like they've got nowhere to go, and I'm walking like some speed walker, looking like a complete dork. People would laugh and heckle."

Dave didn't mind the reputation, though. There were worse prison legacies.

Chase and Dave lived in what Dave calls a "democratic cell." Unlike living with Rusty, Dave and Chase made choices together about their cell. It was acceptable for both cellmates to ask for time in the room. Before moving in together, they talked for weeks about their expectations.

Dave remembers the hardest day he spent in prison. One of his favorite uncles passed away, and Dave couldn't attend the funeral, something that still chokes him up. Chase respected Dave's time to mourn over letters and photographs he spread throughout the cell. He even kept watch in the dayroom to prevent people from coming into their cell.

Chase avoided interacting with cops because he feared sentence elongation. Dave, by contrast, liked to antagonize cops, which made Chase nervous.

"He had done so many years that the entertainment value of messing with the cops was something he was completely over," Dave told me. "It used to cause a little bit of stress to him that I'd be walking with him and I'd give the police a hard time."

Chase had the experience and sense to recognize when others were on the cusp of making fatal mistakes in prison.

"That guy is like a guy in a car going 100 m.p.h., and he's

only about 50 feet away from smashing right into a brick wall." Chase told Dave. "You're trying to help him or give him some advice, but the crash is unavoidable. The only good thing for you to do is make sure you aren't between the car and the brick wall when the wreck happens."

Chase was a proponent for laying low because, after all, no one in prison ever got into trouble for lying on his bunk and reading a book.

"When in doubt, I would remember some people simply cannot be helped until after they get into the disaster they bring upon themselves," Dave said. "So, it was essential for me to pick my moments to help others as best I could.

Chase lives several hours away from me. I first friended him on Facebook and we later corresponded via email. Dave and I laughed about some of the pictures on Chase's page. One shows Chase posing on a tricycle. He posts many TikTok videos, in many of them he is dressed as Batman.

As cellmates, their biggest arguments were over Dave's "Chewbacca" yells he made in the morning when stretching, along with the fact that Dave's feet hung off the bed, which creeped Chase out. There is a child-like innocence to their friendship.

"In prison, you don't want to be social with everybody," Chase wrote me. "In fact, (Dave) pretty much broke every social rule in prison. He reminded me of a big, clumsy Great Dane that meant well, but just kept getting into shit wherever he went."

Dave felt the need to walk up to near-strangers, remind them of their problems, and offer his unsolicited advice, Chase said.

"Not a very smart thing to do in prison," Chase said. "Don't be intrusive and don't make people feel stupid. Again, most of the time he didn't mean to, but he really nailed it most of the time. There wasn't a week that went by where two or three people didn't come up and tell me that my cellie was a big nerd."

Although many thought Dave was a nerd, they used it to their advantage.

"But in all fairness, at least ten or fifteen people a week came and asked him for his help when it came to appeals and write-ups and back problems," Chase said. "I'm not sure he knew what he was talking about, but he sure sounded like he did."

Chase likes to use metaphors.

"The funny thing about Dave: if he was standing on the railroad tracks, he can tell you every little detail about the train coming at him and how it works and the history of trains all together," Chase wrote me. "But it would never occur to him to get the fuck off the tracks. He's one of the most intelligent people I've ever met and yet equally clueless at the same time."

Chase recognizes that coming off as smart can be hazardous in prison, but Dave is smart.

"I can take an almanac and give a specific date and he can tell me what in history was happening on that date," Chase wrote me. "He can tell you about how almost anything works, whether you asked or not. He is nice to have around if you want a quick answer or to spell something right."

Dave's father and brother are pilots, and Dave has his pilot's license. He loved to point out planes to Chase.

"He is definitely not the type of individual that I used to hang out with, but he has a way of growing on you," Chase said. "And I believe we're going to be friends for life—just don't ask him anything about planes. It will never end."

———

SD

I met SD at a Karibou Coffee. He asked that we talk outside so we would have more privacy. SD runs a self-made entertainment group. He spent 11 years in prison after killing someone in self-defense during a home invasion. He first came to Dave to fix a pinched nerve in his neck.

SD had more to worry about than a pinched nerve when first interacting with Dave.

"You know in prison there's a lot of racial tension and racial politics, so for me, once I see a white guy in prison that interacts with black people and different races, it lets me know that he's cool," SD said, "that he's not a dick. Once I found that out, I decided to go talk to him. We sat down and had a real intellectual conversation."

I asked SD if racial tensions made it harder to be Dave's friend.

"Not with me because I'm a leader, and I create my own destiny," SD said. "I create my own path. I'm my own best friend, so can't no one tell me nothing because I don't follow. For me, I live in a world of negative versus positive, real versus fake. I don't see nothing else."

Naturally gregarious, SD told me he doesn't like to live life worrying about boundaries. He has a magnetic personality and describes himself as a people person and typical Aquarius astrological sign.

"Once I seen he was willing to be cool with somebody like me," SD said, "it's nothing to me. I don't care what your friends think. I don't care what my friends think."

SD laughed thinking back to Dave's plan to build a log cabin after his release.

"We used to always talk about what we were going to do when we got out, our plans and stuff like that, getting our life back together, building our foundation, putting our negativity behind us after we served our debt to society and moving forward," SD said.

SD never failed to make fun of the janky little cabin models Dave constructed out of rolled up pieces of papier-mâché, called sticks. Dave still fantasizes about moving to a secluded cabin in the woods.

SD told me that white people in prison are much more concerned with policing their race.

"They don't want you sitting with us," SD said about white people not wanting to sit with people of other races. "They don't want you talking to us. They don't want you eating with us. They don't want you conversing with us. So, they're going to feel some type of way. They're going to look at you like a rebellion against your own race."

Black prisoners aren't policed to the same extent by other black prisoners, but always have to think about racism coming from others, SD said.

"This right here has been a burn to us our whole life," SD pointed to his skin. "It's systematic, so we're kinda aware of our surroundings and stuff like that, but I'm not going to act funny to you because you're white."

I asked SD what he thought about Dave's friendships with

people in white supremacist prison gangs. SD described it as inevitable.

"Just because I have a shitty cellie or have a negative cellie don't mean I have to be like that," SD said.

SD has the ethos of a true businessman and respects that Dave had to make connections. He recognizes that this must have caused problems along the way.

"I see it as a territorial thing," SD said. "He's being territorial. He's adapting to his environment, so him as a white man, he's supposed to have white friends. That's just life."

SD also attributed Dave's adaptation to economic and class differences.

"Dave was raised as an upper middle-class white man," SD said. "So, he's suburbs. He's never lived in where I come from. He never came from poverty. He never came from the streets, the grain of the gutter. So, him being that, of course he's going to automatically adapt to stuff like that when it comes his way. At the same time, Doc's a very smart individual, so he doesn't see color. Now I'm not going to say once upon a time in his life it hasn't crossed his mind. I don't know that it has. I don't like putting jackets on people. I'm not going to put a jacket on that man because I don't know that part of that man. I just know from what I know of him."

I asked SD if he sees Dave as racist.

"This is what I honestly believe: I believe any white person of a particular age has a lot of biases," SD said. "I believe that if you're a white man in this world and you come from a particular background, I believe that you have a slight, little bit of racism. Now it can be prejudices, it can be bigotry, or a little bit of racism. I don't know which one, but I believe you have a little bit of that in you."

SD demands respect, but recognizes the cultural differences between him and Dave.

"He's a 50-year-old, white man," SD said. "He come from

parents who probably hate people. I'm not going to let that stop our friendship. I like Dave. I genuinely like Dave, so I'm not going to let that affect my life because I feel like Dave and I can become millionaires together. I hate racism, but I don't let it affect how I put my pants on every day. I don't let it affect me getting to my money or becoming a successful entrepreneur."

Now, SD helps Dave with his tree work business. He is excited to go fishing, camping, and attend basketball games together.

SD, looking relaxed and looking good as always.

"My future is so bright you need glasses," SD told me. "I'm a very opinionated person. I'm career oriented. I'm the life of the party sometimes. I'm an all-around good guy. I speak my mind. I don't hold my tongue for nothing. I'll tell you when something's not right. I'm not a yes man. I'm a mogul in the making."

A self-described family man, SD strives to accumulate wealth within the next five years. He works as a rapper, producer, composer, and promoter for his entertainment company. He also plans to write a guidebook on how to love an incarcerated man. SD is planning to create documentaries and is releasing an album coming out next year. He will get off parole in about two years.

"I love being out," SD said. "I love my freedom. I hate jail with a passion. That's what you call for me a life-changing experience. That was my first time in prison and my last time in prison. I will never go back. It was an amazing experience for me. It taught me a lot. It grew me up a lot. Gave me a lot of wisdom, knowledge, taught me patience. It let me see who's who. Prison for me was a gift and a curse."

Although SD did take lessons away from prison, he doesn't believe his sentence needed to be over a decade long, noting that prisons are a waste of taxpayer money.

Many fathers are incarcerated, which adds extra pressure on mothers. SD has considerable respect for his wife, who is also a mother. She married SD while he was incarcerated.

"It takes a certain type of human being to do that," SD said. "She was there with me all 11 years I was in prison. She had my back mentally, physically, financially, and spiritually. It takes a certain type of human being. I call her superwoman."

Holidays

One of the first questions I had for Dave was what he did during holidays. He told me that his friends and family were sadder for him then he was for himself. He often wrote letters during the holidays to reassure them he was well.

Dave also knew it was a tense time for people serving long sentences.

"About a week before Thanksgiving, people start acting very strange, especially people who have children or people who have sick parents or anything like that," Dave said. "Starting a week or two before Thanksgiving, I would just shut down all my interaction with people I didn't know just because people freak out."

Dave and his cellmates strove to make the best of the holidays. He received care packages filled with better-quality snacks from his dad. With the contents of the care package, and whatever else they could scrounge up, Dave celebrated the 12 days of Christmas. Each day he and his cellie pulled out a treat to share.

"One thing that happens when you get a bunch of guys

together, and I think it's really similar to guys at war, if you're deployed to combat and it's Christmas, everyone knows it sucks," Dave said. "People were really good at not mentioning it. Everyone does the best they can to keep the mood as light-hearted as possible."

Dave felt like a kid during Christmas because he got to watch *Charlie Brown Christmas*, *Rudolph the Red Nose Reindeer*, and NFL football on T.V. He ramped up the banter with cops, pretending like he knew about a staff holiday party, and the cop wasn't invited.

"Every Christmas I had in was a good day for me," Dave said. "That was a time that I felt really guilty about my family because cards started coming in and cousins and people I didn't speak to very often and everybody would say the same thing."

They thought it was terrible he was in prison. Dave felt guilty because it wasn't terrible.

"I was sure to let them know that Christmas was a time of happiness, and that I was getting together with other guys to celebrate the holidays," Dave said. "I wrote to them about feasts we shared on Thanksgiving and about the parties that we threw for birthdays."

But Dave omitted certain traditions from his letters.

"I left out the part about the birthday boy being beaten on by his friends, as tradition dictated," Dave said.

Birthdays were posted on each cell door alongside D.O.C. numbers, so all knew when to celebrate. Birthday celebrations were comprised of a big feast and a light beating. Dave assured me the older guys weren't badly beaten. Everyone showed up at the cell in question, armed with snacks like sausages or chips. Together, they made burritos or nachos with the pooled ingredients.

"Birthdays were a joyous time," Dave said.

———

Teaching

Each of the three prisons in which Dave spent time had a different level of security. The changes were most glaring in the medium-level prison, Sterling. Each cell had personal keys to the doors and drywall instead of brick. The cell key was a belonging that Dave actually had to worry about losing.

"I felt like a free man," Dave said. "It was really weird because I could walk outside at night. I hadn't seen a star, other than through the little arrow-slit windows, for over a year."

When he arrived, Dave walked out on the grass and took off his boots and socks.

The cops told him to put his shoes back on.

"It's the little things like that that really felt like freedom because it was a step in the right direction," Dave said.

Dave knew that it was one of the most violent prisons in Colorado, especially on its high security side. It had a triple fence perimeter with two metal chain link fences with barbed wire around the top. The bottom was lined with razor wire, so aspiring escapees couldn't dig underneath it. The middle fence was an electrified fence powerful enough to kill.

Dave took a prison job at Sterling as a G.E.D. tutor. Officer Tamayo, whom Dave describes as a "jerk," oversaw the tutoring operation. Initially, the prison was receptive to Dave because of his own background as a high school teacher. Members of a prominent Southside gang often took the tutoring classes to receive their G.E.D. Dave explained to me that Southside gang members are required to be educated. Dave helped students complete their homework, but made it clear he wouldn't do it for them. Dave also felt an obligation to help the Southside members because of his loose association with Rusty, a member of an opposing gang.

"If it turns into a war between our two gangs there's going to be a massive problem, so let's just be cool," Dave told me. "We can do business together."

Despite his loose affiliation with Rusty, Dave still respects the Southside gang. He thinks it commendable that they value education. He admires their ability to keep their business private.

"They were great," Dave told me. "Even the young guys and the new guys really walked a straight line because they were very swift and severe with punishing their own. I liked them."

The Southside shot-caller on the low side of Sterling was one of Dave's students. He wondered why he actually had to do assignments and couldn't just pay Dave off to do it for him.

Dave's response: "Because I respect you and I respect education. For me to just do your work for you means I don't think you're smart enough to do it. And I would not insult you by telling you I think you're too stupid to do your work and just do it for you."

The leader looked at Dave with his tattooed face and replied, "But I'm a criminal."

Dave didn't care.

Officer Tomayo, on the other hand, disliked the fact that Dave was grading their papers with pencil so they wouldn't fail. Dave and the students later worked through the problems together.

"I thought, I'm either going to piss off a cop or I'm going to piss off an inmate," Dave said. "Any time there's a situation where you can piss off one or the other, you always have to piss off the cop. Because they show up pissed off."

Dave defended himself, emphasizing that it was his job to help students succeed. He pointed out that there was no real difference between him and Officer Tomayo, except Dave was at the lowest point in his life while she was at the peak of her career, and he was far more adept at teaching.

"Some jobs, such as G.E.D. tutor, made leg-riding almost a requirement of the job since tutors often worked in unison with the teachers," Dave said. "The teachers all held the rank of lieutenant or above and were cops even though they wore civilian clothing. One of the reasons I was so defiant to my teacher-boss was to remove any speculation that I might be a leg-rider."

The students in the class loved Dave's response. Officer Tamayo, not so much. Dave knew he would get written up for his refusal to follow a direct order, a class two offense. Officer Tamayo told Dave to either work for her husband in the dish pit or go to ad seg in handcuffs until his hearing; if found guilty he would go straight to the dish pit. Dave knew the result would be the same either way. The bulk of those written up were found guilty.

When Dave arrived to work in the dish pit, members of the same Southside gang ran the kitchen. Used meal trays were stored in the dish pit for rinsing and putting through the industrial dishwasher. The dish pit is considered the worst job in the facility. They gave Dave a hard time, delegating him to stand in the corner and work the hose without talking. Dave told them to consult with his tutoring students. They were confused as to why Dave had been transferred and was throwing around their shot-caller's name. When they heard the story, they were incredulous that Dave had actually raised his voice to a teacher. Dave continued to tutor his former students on the side. He was soon released from the dish pit and moved up the kitchen hierarchy.

Dave once taught me something that helped him endure without succumbing to bitterness: he consciously decided not to think about hypothetical situations in which he experienced less prison time.

Dave doesn't change the realities of his situation, but rather his perspective. He was imprisoned by a private prison company; therefore, once he had an opening with his bus accident, he sued that private prison company.

"I don't know if it's the healthiest point of view in the world, but it sure made my days go by faster," Dave said.

He calls it flipping the script.

7

Department of Confinement

"The LORD will fight for you; you need only to be still."
Exodus 14:14

Dave with Brie. This is a photo Dave mailed to a friend while
in prison and still hangs on his refrigerator.

"I refused to call it Department of Corrections," Dave told me
once. "I called it the Department of Confinement. The only
thing they're good at is confining people, and they were really
good at confining people. The corrections part of it is almost
completely non-existent, unless they take it upon themselves."

Dave has a sort of youthful defiance.

"Constantly harassing the cops—that was one of my pastimes," Dave said. "Not so much that I would get into trouble. If you're going to incarcerate me, you're going to have to put up with me."

While working in the kitchen, Dave enjoyed slamming heavy trays against the stainless-steel counters while Officer Charlesworth conducted orientations for new hires.

Dave liked Officer Charlesworth. He managed the property room in which Dave picked up his National Geographic and Audubon Society magazines. Officer Charlesworth always hassled Dave about returning his old ones.

"I get Audubon magazine," Dave told Officer Charlesworth. "I'm a nerd. I read about bird watching. This is not a problem. You want everybody in their room, laying down, reading about bird watching. One cop could run the whole prison if everyone was laying down and reading about bird watching. Why are you gonna take my magazine? You get paid the exact same amount of money, whether you're cool or a dick. It's the same paycheck; and it's easier to be cool."

If Dave gave cops trouble, he liked them.

"Some of them were very nice people," Dave said. "I have no idea why they wanted that career. Charlesworth was a very nice person; he just over compensated. He thought he had to come across as a jerk."

However, Dave could never become super close with them.

"The cops were universally regarded by everyone—other than the snitches and leg-riders—as the enemy," Dave told me. "A leg-rider is an inmate who seeks to gain safety by always staying close to the cops. Leg-riders were also universally loathed, though not hated to quite the extent of a known snitch."

Cops lost respect by being quick to write COPDs or by maintaining an uptight attitude.

"Cops who gave overly thorough pat-downs—often

involving rough treatment of testicles—were pricks," Dave said. "One such cop at Sterling had a huge bushy mustache, so we dubbed him 'porn-stache.' If an inmate came back to the living unit in a sullen mood, he could explain his disposition to the guys in the day room by saying something like, 'I just got nutted by porn-stache' and everyone would understand that he was grumpy and wanted to be left alone. Otherwise, having an overly sour disposition in the living unit was frowned upon since it affected the morale of the other guys."

Officer Shields at Burlington became notorious by giving overly thorough shakedowns. Shields wore tight pants, which earned him the reputation of being gay. Dave told me that the culture in prison wasn't much more tolerant than 1950s society. Shields enjoyed throwing personal belongings around during shakedowns, often breaking items and creating large messes. During said shakedowns, he smiled and told Dave to enjoy putting his room back together.

Dave smiles thinking about the day when Shields accidentally sprayed himself with pepper spray. He was sitting in the glass security bubble at the time. He wasn't permitted to leave the bubble unattended; he sat in his own gas chamber until the alarm triggered an activation from the special operations response team. The SORT team wore battle fatigues, including helmets and shields.

"We all had a good laugh as Shields was hauled off by the SORT with tears and snot covering his face," Dave said. "Shields was a world-class idiot."

A sergeant at Sterling who worked in the chow hall was an older woman nicknamed Big Bird. She stood about 6'2,"—had a long pointy nose, prominent bulging eyes, and yellow-tinted, gray hair. She was infamous for writing guys up for taking too long to finish their meal beyond the 20-minute allotment; she hovered over tables and chastised the guys in question," Dave explained.

"We called her Big-Bird because she really did look like the Sesame Street character," Dave said. "No one liked Big Bird very much, but she wasn't more than an annoyance unless someone talked back to her. Back-talking Big-Bird was a sure way to get a write-up."

Officer Frost at Delta was infamous for conducting overly thorough strip searches. After visiting hours, Frost conducted a humiliating strip search before Dave could return to the living unit. The visiting room is one of the places where contraband is most likely to be introduced to the facility, but Frost was always a little too eager. COs weren't allowed to touch people in the nude, but they thoroughly examined them with flashlights and asked them to cough. Dave enjoyed razzing Frost, asking him if he enjoyed telling his wife and kids how seriously he took the strip searches.

"I always felt a little ashamed of myself for berating the COs, but it was part of my way of not allowing myself to be beaten down by the experience," Dave said. "And, it helped my cred amongst the other inmates. Old-timers would come up to me on the rec yard and ask if it was true, if I had told Frost I was showing how much I respected him by spreading my cheeks."

The old-timers approved.

"They would howl in laughter when I nodded and ask how I didn't get written up in a disciplinary report. The old-timers would just kind of nod as if they understood how I went about fighting the cage in my own way—by flipping the script. If they were going to incarcerate me, they were going to have to know how I felt about them."

Frost subsequently delegated the strip search to another officer, who conducted the protocol with more respect and decorum.

"Most of the COs were pretty polite," Dave told me. "They knew I wasn't going to cause any trouble for them, so they treated me with a measure of respect. And, in return, I was always certain to let them know that I knew they were in charge and that I would do what I was supposed to do. 'Don't start nothing, won't be nothing' is some prison slang that is often repeated whenever any type of conflict seems to be evident. And, it is almost always true. In truth, I felt sorry for most of the COs. What a terrible job."

Dave told me some other lines used on COs who tested him:

"They had to drag me here in hand-cuffs and leg shackles," Dave said. "They have to put up a razor wire fence and electrify it to keep me in here. That's how bad this place sucks. But you, you drove here today on purpose. I bet you have enough gas in your car to make it to a resort up in the mountains, a vacation paradise. I bet your car has a steering wheel that allows you to make it take you wherever you want to go. You could be anywhere you want to be, but you chose to be in here with me, today. And, you'll probably make the same choice tomorrow, too. Man, that's really sad. So, please don't be rude to me because you hate the choices you have made."

Dave still feels chagrin thinking of cops provoking his cruelty.

"A better person would just ignore them, I thought," Dave said. "A better person would just turn the other cheek. But I felt like I had to stick up for myself. And, I usually only had to give a hard time to a CO once for him to stay clear of me and allow me to mind my own business."

While in prison, Dave learned that cops and the D.O.C. were often incompetent. ICE questioned Dave while he was in prison. Born in Spain because of his father's service in the Air Force, the D.O.C. record keepers thought Dave was a Spanish national. Dave's case manager notified him that D.O.C. was trying to deport him to Spain. When ICE officers met Dave, they soon deduced that Dave was a U.S. citizen.

———

Prison Labor

One of the key arguments against prisons is that the labor conducted is tantamount to slavery; prisoners often get wages equaling less than a dollar per hour. Dave agreed that some prison jobs, are in fact, unfair labor. He saw cases of guys contracted by cities to maintain various public spaces like parks.

"If you're mowing a yard at a city park, there's some high school kid who works at the city that should have that job and be making a decent wage," Dave told me. "The fact that a street person should have that job and these guys were willing to do it, it seemed to me that that is bordering on slavery, especially because money gets skimmed by the prison."

Dave adopted an attitude of civil disobedience, which he defines as: "If you don't believe in the system, find a way to fight against the system that doesn't lead to you getting punished more."

At the kitchen in Delta, prep cooks and bakers were locked in a small room while handling knives. The COs kept track of these tools easier if they were confined to a smaller area. Ventilation in the knife area was notoriously limited, with the only source of fresh air coming from the heating and air conditioning vents, which were often turned off. During fall, a nasty smell emitted from the heating units due to the dust and other debris collected while sitting idle throughout the summer. Bakers complained about the smell of exhaust in the bakery and reported being light-headed and feeling sick while at work. The captain responsible for the kitchen put in a maintenance request and the lieutenant of the facility sent a crew to inspect the heater.

The inspection revealed elevated levels of carbon monoxide, but they determined that the levels were still within the "safe" range. The inspection was conducted while the heaters were off.

The captain decided that the cooks could continue to work in the small room. Bakers reported increased symptoms and were growing agitated. The captain and lieutenant called an outside contractor to perform another inspection. Again, elevated levels of carbon monoxide were discovered, but were also deemed "safe." The next day, a baker named Alex passed out.

"I could see him lying completely still on the floor, directly under the vent from the heater," Dave told me. "I alerted the COs, and they immediately opened the door to the bakery and dragged Alex, who was completely unconscious and unresponsive, to the back-loading dock for the kitchen outside."

Alex looked lifeless on the back-loading dock. He lacked a pulse and wasn't breathing. One of the COs, a paramedic prior to being employed by the D.O.C, immediately began to perform CPR until the civilian ambulance came and whisked Alex to the local hospital.

"All of us kitchen workers formed a relatively tight-knit group," Dave said. "We all pitched in to help when a fellow worker was having a bad day. And we all worked together to make special meals and snacks to share when the COs weren't looking. For us to see Alex lying lifeless on the loading dock was a distressing experience. Our anger toward the captain, who was not a very likable person to begin with, grew to the point that we felt genuine hatred for the lack of concern she showed toward our well-being. But we remained silent other than the whispers between us over our disgust at her behavior and our silent prayers that Alex would pull through and be okay."

Always doing the work of one-and-a-half people, Alex was a popular member of the crew. He smuggled in dough and other ingredients to make everyone cinnamon rolls. At the end of his sentence, he spoke positively about his family and how he was excited to see them.

Dave said for them to watch a friend and co-worker loaded

into an ambulance was horrible. They could discern from the CO's body language that the situation was dire.

"We were completely powerless to help, but that is the instinct that we shared," Dave said. "So, we were all frustrated, angry, and scared for our friend and co-worker."

As per policy, the COs provided no updates on Alex's condition. Several days passed, and no one knew if he were alive. Informed that the carbon monoxide levels were now considered to be severely high, to the point of being life-threatening, inspectors discovered a hole in the exhaust hose of the heating unit. This allowed exhaust to pour into the vent that supplied air to the bakery. As the tests were only conducted when the heating unit was off, these increased levels were not detected.

"We were outraged at the stupidity and carelessness of the COs," Dave said. "It seemed so obvious to us that there would be greater risk of carbon monoxide poisoning when the unit was turned on rather than off."

Alex returned to a hero's welcome about four days later. Dave thought he was probably sore from all the pats on the back, strong fist-bumps, firm handshakes, and even a few hugs —a rarity in a men's prison. He talked about being brought back to life in the ambulance with the paramedics' shock paddles, along with his stay in the ICU where he breathed through a respirator to help flush the carbon monoxide from his system. He bragged about the attractive nurses who cared for him in the civilian hospital. And, amazingly, he was back on the weight yard the day after he returned, as was his routine. Already unpopular because she fed people smaller portions than deemed essential by the official D.O.C. nutritionist, the captain's reputation became even more unfavorable.

Dave didn't hold back in comparing the captain to Hitler: "What historical figure is known for underfeeding his prisoners, then locking them in chambers filled with poisonous gas? That is exactly how us kitchen guys feel about you, captain."

In the aftermath, Dave inculcated in himself the principle that COs were a part of the prison itself.

"I remembered going to the zoo as a kid and seeing a newly captured tiger repeatedly throwing himself against the steel bars of his cage," Dave told me. "He was torturing himself, injuring himself mentally, physically, and—I guessed—emotionally as well, by bashing into a steel cage over and over, again. By thinking of the COs as part of the cage, I found some peace in how I dealt with them."

Rather than arguing and losing his temper, Dave took a different approach.

"I would remind them that, to me, they weren't even human —that they were nothing more than a part of the cage," Dave said.

Dave also reminded them that he would be gone within a few years or months, as time wound down. They, on the other hand "-would still be a part of the cage long after I was gone," Dave said.

Although Dave maintained his civil disobedience, he balanced it with a sense of caution for losing what little freedoms he had.

"I could walk out, get horseshoes and play horseshoes in the grass," Dave said. "That's a pretty nice freedom compared to not being able to walk outside, and when you do walk outside it's just a concrete courtyard, which has big walls you can't see out. It's just like being in a living unit except there's no roof. No one wanted to break rules so badly that they would go to the high side. Unless they were in a gang and for some reason or another they wanted to be on the high side."

———

Huevos Porcelana

Dave enjoyed huevos porcelana. To eat this prison delicacy, Dave stuffed boiled eggs in his baggy pants while in the walk-in refrigerator, which wasn't surveyed by a camera. While in the privacy of the bathroom, Dave ate his eggs while sitting on his porcelain seat.

"I used to have a $300 check at a restaurant for taking the staff out, and fresh salads and a bottle of wine," Dave said about his chiropractor days. "Now I'm eating hard-boiled eggs on a freaking toilet wearing my pajamas. Man, this is just one of those telling moments."

Dave told me many stories about how stealing food was one of the best ways to beat the system. It was also necessary for needed calories, as the prison diet was extremely minimal.

"I'm a pretty big guy, and I have a high metabolism," Dave said. "They didn't feed us enough. So, to be able to have half a dozen hard-boiled eggs during a work shift made a big difference. When I would get home to my cell, I wouldn't have to cook things out of my box. Of course, I always had food in my footlocker because I never wanted to be hungry."

Dave and others usually kept a full box of extra food. Rumors sometimes circulated that cooks on the high side of the prison sent over food contaminated by something vile over to the low side. No one ate from the cafeteria on those days, instead dipping into their food reserves.

Guys were always thinking of ways to steal food and smuggle it back to the housing unit—a risky operation. Foods that were easier to steal included hard-boiled eggs, little trays of carrots, celery sticks, along with bananas or apples. Dave remembers stuffing hamburger patties wrapped in saran wrap to the seat of Munch's wheelchair. Named because of his protruding teeth that stuck out even when he closed his mouth, Munch was "somewhat deplorable" in Dave's estimation. He had drug addiction issues and was in prison for killing a baby. He was someone with whom Dave could steal food; befriending him was out of the question.

Altering uniforms served as a way of fostering individuality in the sea of identical jumpsuits. One gang wore uniforms with three seams down the back. Dave had one seam sewn on his to signify he was on good terms with them and they wanted him to have a sharp-looking uniform for visits. Dave snuck a full set of greens, a brown overcoat, and a pair of boots out of the prison.

"I wanted to have it in my closet as a reminder," Dave told me. "It's kinda humbling."

8

Bees

"*Do not be afraid of those who kill the body but cannot kill the soul. Rather, be afraid of the One who can destroy both soul and body in hell.*"
Matthew 10:28

Burlington had a major lockdown twice a year. With everything closed for a week, officers went through every cell, combing through belongings. They searched for drugs, tattoo needles, and weapons, among other things. With the lockdown in effect, inmates couldn't work in the kitchen. Corrections officers ran the kitchen for that week. Disregarding safety and sanitation, many of the inmates got sick. Dave and his cellmate at the time, Bo, both caught the stomach flu.

"Bo was a great guy," Dave told me. "We got along very well, thank goodness. But it's a seven-by-ten concrete box. Two guys. One stainless steel toilet. We were each throwing up so bad and had diarrhea so bad that it was one of those things when I could look at it and say that was the absolute low point of my entire life. Because here he's sitting on it. He gets up to go about his business and I had to stick my face in it. And I'm just as sick as you can imagine."

At that point, Dave looked at Bo and asked if things could possibly get worse. Bo responded that things could indeed get worse if there were bees attacking them during their bouts with the stomach flu.

"Any time I was having a really bad day, which happened every now and again, I would think okay it could be worse, I could be getting stung by bees on top of everything else, and I would think about how the only thing that could really make it worse is to add getting stung by bees," Dave said.

In the original Craigslist ad that Dave posted for an author, he described his experiences beyond prison. I feel a little bad that this book mostly focused on prison because Dave has had a life replete with challenge, but also dynamism. Those prior experiences helped Dave mentally overcome the hardships faced in prison.

"They could take away my pilot's license, but they couldn't take away my memories of flying," Dave said. "They could take away my chiropractor's license, but they couldn't take away my desire to help others. They could take away my bicycles, but not my passion for cycling. They could remove me from my friends and family, but they couldn't decrease the love I have for them all. They could refer to me as #166054, but they couldn't keep me from being a father, son, brother, cousin, friend, doctor, pilot, cyclist, student, teacher, or anything else that defines who I am."

Dave experienced a multitude of daunting challenges, including fear of physical altercations with people in the prison.

"I soon realized that the mental and emotional aspects of being incarcerated were going to be far more challenging than the physical aspects," Dave said. "So, I started to look for strategies to maintain a positive frame of mind."

He soon realized that there were no emails to check, no

phones to monitor, no sales calls from telemarketers to avoid, no rude drivers, no bills to pay, and no deadlines in general.

"My life had been such a chaotic mess in the months leading up to my incarceration that, for the first time in over a year, I could completely relax and be at peace," Dave said.

Dave took a new approach to the physical constraints around him.

"I viewed the walls, bars, and fences as protection from the outside world and its many challenges," Dave said. "Rather than view the physical prison as a cage to keep me in, I viewed it as a castle designed to shield me from the outside world."

This is where flipping the script came into play. It's now one of Dave's favorite mottos.

"Any time something bad happened to me or to a buddy, I would try to figure out how it could be turned into a positive," Dave said. "It wasn't always possible, but it worked most of the time."

The Cycle of Life

For the bulk of Dave's undergraduate college years, he identified as a cyclist more than as a student. It led to his decision to major in exercise physiology at the University of Florida, where he received his B.S. in 1992 and his M.S. in 1995. Members of the faculty, Dr. Cade, the inventor of Gatorade, and Arthur Jones, the inventor of Nautilus fitness equipment, inspired Dave both in school and as a cyclist. Dave was the first Florida rider to win an S.E.C. championship. You can Wikipedia "Team Florida Cycling" to see a photo of young Dave celebrating the day. Two Pro-Am teams made Dave offers after the race. For some years, Dave "muddled through" before realizing that he was talented enough to hang in the pack through tough races, but nowhere near good enough to earn a living at the sport.

During Dave's first year of collegiate racing, a crash left him with a broken arm and a broken nose. The x-ray resembled crunched up potato chips instead of a human hand, with 17 total fractures in his hand, wrist and arm. His six-week recovery was miserable.

"I missed the exercise," Dave said. "I missed my teammates. I missed being able to roll through the north Florida countryside and feel the freedom that comes from enjoying youth and fitness and friendships. I felt incarcerated, in a way."

Dave had a comeback, of sorts, at 35. Now able to compete in the master's racing category, participants were passionate, but not showy. He didn't have to worry about big crashes as much. In 2004, Dave competed in the Florida State Championship road race. In peak physical form after intense training, Dave hoped to place. The course suited his abilities with a mixture of rolling hills and long flat sections on rough roads—typical north Florida terrain. The weather was cold and rainy, which suited him, too. The conditions weren't ideal for South Florida riders who don't enjoy rough roads or bad weather. The race was 75 miles, five laps around a fifteen-mile circuit. On the first lap, Dave removed his clear racing glasses to wipe grit from his face and dropped them when he hit a pothole. Riding the rest of the race without eye protection, racers kicked up road grit and wetness into Dave's eyes.

"It's a mess," Dave told me. "By the end of the race, I was drenched, cold, tired from the efforts, and nearly blind from what seemed like a pound of sand filling each of my eye sockets. I didn't have it in me to contest for the sprint finish and ended up finishing in 17th place."

Dave knew he could stop at several points and the warm team bus would be waiting with hot soup and stiff whiskey drinks inside.

"Compared to the cold, wet misery I was feeling on the bike, being in the bus would have felt like being in a king's royal chamber," Dave said. "I wrestled with the idea of abandoning the race, but instead thought about how much better those luxuries would be after one more lap around the brutal circuit. So, I pressed on. And, I was right. Enduring the brief hardship of another 40 minutes of racing did make the reward much more enjoyable."

Starting with 100 guys, Dave finished with the remaining 40 racers.

"Like all endurance athletes, I learned how to suffer in silence," Dave said. "No one ever complained about the weather because we were all in the same situation. Guys who didn't see the point in pushing through it just climbed off of their bikes and into their vans or busses. In prison, I vowed to never complain about the conditions. All of us prisoners were in the same situation, so there was no point in griping about the bad food, the shortages of toilet paper, the length of a sentence or anything else—with one exception: we all griped about what assholes some of the corrections officers could be. That was the only thing a prisoner could complain about without coming across as a whiner. And, no one likes a whiner."

Dave remembered that rainy bike ride when he had hard days in prison.

"I remember thinking on days that were really hard or frustrating in prison, this is still a lot easier than that day on the bike," Dave said. "I've been through worse."

Now, prison is like that rainy bike ride memory.

"I have a car and I have money and I can go to a restaurant or a movie," Dave said. "Having the experience of being in for five years makes challenges seem less significant now, which is good."

As I got to know Dave and found out that he had been through significant personal turmoil before prison, I was relieved in a perverse way. I think he needed those hard times to have an easier time while locked away.

———

Flying

Dave's father and brother are pilots. At 21, Dave took steps to obtain his pilot's license. The final step toward being eligible for his check-ride with an FAA examiner was a long solo cross-country flight, covering over 500 miles and landing at a minimum of three airports. Dave started at Andrews Air Force Base in Maryland and landed in Farmville, Virginia.

Aptly named, the town's landscape was mostly farms, making it difficult to land. Proficient at instrument navigation using radio beacons and referencing his position on the aviation charts, Dave executed a good landing. He refueled the Cessna 152, which Dave thought of as a little more than an aluminum kite with a lawnmower engine.

The weather forecast was clear to Hampton, Virginia—the next landing point of his trip. Located on a coastline, Dave landed easily.

His flight back to Andrews was the final step in becoming a fully licensed private pilot. The Flight Service Station told Dave of a band of thunderstorms spanning the entire width of the state; these conditions would make it nearly impossible to fly. He saw a thick cloud cover with some gaps between the building storms that he could sneak through if the storms got too dangerous. Despite the weatherperson's advice to wait until the storms passed, Dave carried on because he was worried about making it home before dark. Dave flew about 1,000 feet underneath the clouds that grew increasingly darker above him.

"Flying underneath the clouds in a thunderstorm in a small aircraft is a terrifying experience," Dave told me. "There was rain pelting the canopy. There was lightning flashing to my left and right, and—it seemed—above and below me, too. The turbulence from the storm was tossing my small plane around like a hummingbird in a hurricane. I was terrified. I was also cursing myself for allowing my enthusiasm to distort my thinking and lead to such an irrational string of decisions."

The storm forced Dave to descend lower and lower in an effort to maintain some forward visibility. Flying at about 300 feet above ground, Dave searched for visual landmarks. Using the radio navigational aids was impossible as he used both hands on the controls to keep the wings level.

"I was wrestling with a thunderstorm, a losing proposition in such a small airplane," Dave said.

Eventually, Dave spotted a recognizable landmark and he emerged from the thunderstorms and landed in Andrews.

"The lesson I reflected on often was when in doubt, it is often best to do absolutely nothing," Dave said. "It is better to wait out a storm while safely on the ground. That lesson served me well in prison."

As Dave became better at seeing brewing trouble, he became better at avoiding it.

"No one ever got into trouble for lying on their bunk and reading a book is something I reminded myself of every day," Dave said. "I would think of my bunk as being the Hampton airport, a place I should have stayed for an evening and enjoyed. In prison, even a small riot or gang fight is something that cannot be steered around, ducked under or climbed over. The only way to be safe is to be far away from it when it kicks off. Such fights happen very rarely, but it only takes being involved in one for something catastrophic to happen. Airplane crashes happen very rarely, too, but the results are usually equally catastrophic."

Dave remembers thinking he might crash while flying several times. Once was while with his brother, who didn't realize how little power a small airplane has compared to commercial-sized jets. On another occasion, Dave and his uncle nearly flew into a mountain. And yet another time, his uncle showed him how to go upside down in a little Cessna, not knowing that the engine quits while going upside down. In that instance, the two happened to be flying above an alligator-infested swamp.

"Discretion is the better part of valor," Dave said. "Sun Tzu says in *The Art of War* that one should never fight on indefensible terrain. Never launch an attack uphill or defend against an attack that is coming downhill toward your position."

During the year leading up to Dave's arrest, he experienced a heart attack. While in the ICU for 10 days, Dave thought he might die or lose a leg. With limited experience being hospitalized, Dave had a catheter inserted into his body during surgery. When he woke up, he didn't realize they had done so, a blunt reminder that he didn't have control over his body.

"Whenever things got really crappy, I would remember when I was in the ICU all hooked up," Dave said. "The cycling taught me I could get through a hard day. And the flying taught me that I needed to avoid trouble by getting to a safe place and waiting for the conditions to get better. I don't think I'm exaggerating when I say, I'd rather have a year at Delta than ten days in the ICU. The ICU was just that bad. Having those life experiences gave me coping strategies that were effective in one way or another."

Several months into the project, Dave got news that Bo died in a car accident shortly after his release from prison. Dave was devastated, but will always lovingly conjure Bo's philosophy.

Things could definitely get worse when faced with a bee swarm.

9

No One Does Time Alone

"See the birds of the sky, that they don't sow, neither do they reap, nor gather into barns. Your heavenly Father feeds them. Aren't you of much more value than they?"
Matthew 6:26

When I first met Dave, he told me that no one does time alone. When someone is imprisoned, friends, family members, acquaintances, business partners, and maybe others endure punishment along with the physically incarcerated person. To Dave, this is the most painful reality of imprisonment.

"One thing is true," Dave said. "No one who is incarcerated does their time alone. When I was sentenced, I knew that all of my friends and family had just been sentenced, too, in a way. I knew they would be worried about my physical safety. I knew they would be concerned about my mental well-being. And, I knew that there would be sadness, anger, and confusion felt by a lot of people."

Dave told me of his visitors in prison. He appreciated the gestures and company itself, but worried about the often-dirty visiting room and the strenuous drives to get there. His visitors included Tim, his father, stepmother and brother. Dave also had a girlfriend of less than a year when he first entered prison. He describes his visit with her as terrible—not because he didn't want to see her, but because it was hard to put her in that position.

"It was harder for her than it was for me because she had all this uncertainty," Dave told me.

Dave was relieved when she broke up with him by phone. This was after six months of incarceration. He felt a lingering unease with the possibility that their relationship would have to endure over his 13-year sentence.

"Maybe you can maintain a relationship with someone who is in prison while you are on the outside, but you shouldn't," Dave told her. "Go live your life. And when I get out, we bump into each other or reconnect, whatever, we can write letters. We can pick up where we left off. Maybe the man of your dreams is someone you're going to meet two weeks from now. Who knows? There's just so many maybes. But don't incarcerate yourself on my behalf."

For Dave, time passed far more quickly after the breakup. It hurt knowing that people were in pain because of his situation, especially when Dave had easy days in prison spent playing Scrabble or cards with friends.

"So, I decided to use letters to help assuage any hardships that my loved ones might be experiencing," Dave said. "I wrote often. In every letter, I made sure that everyone knew I was safe and sound and doing well. That was my typical closing sentence in almost every letter. I also made sure to let everyone know that I had everything I needed—that I was eating well, had comfortable and warm clothing, that I was laughing every day, and that I was not at risk of being a victim in any way."

Dave shared humorous stories as well, often likening the

facilities to *One Flew Over the Cuckoo's Nest* rather than *Shaw-shank Redemption, Escape from Alcatraz,* or *American History X.*

Dave wrote about current events, so letter recipients knew he had access to T.V., newspapers, and magazines. He debated politics with them to prove he was still somewhat sharp. He lamented losses by his favorite sports teams and celebrated victories.

"I tried to write in such a way that my loved ones would laugh when they read mail from me," Dave said. "At the same time, I was certain to let them know that even though I wasn't experiencing hard time, I was definitely looking forward to my release date, and that I was doing everything I could to make sure that date came as soon as possible. I would tell them how much I looked forward to seeing them again. And, I would let them know how much getting mail from them lifted my spirits. I wanted them to know how important they are to me and how much I love them. I wanted them to look forward to opening a letter from me when it showed up in their mailbox."

Dave also promised himself to never complain in his letters.

By writing only about the positives, Dave was forced to actively look for more positives, however small, so he could have something new to describe in his letters.

"I wrote about seeing birds flying overhead during seasons of migration," Dave said. "I wrote about how much my life improved when I moved to a lower security-level facility—like walking on grass barefoot once I arrived at Sterling. I wrote about studying aspects of the law and about how I was able to use that knowledge by filing appeals to help guys who had been incorrectly sentenced. I wrote about how I was enjoying having so much free time to devote to introspective thought and about plans I was developing for my comeback story."

With each new prison transfer, Dave wrote letters to everyone in his family and to the friends with whom he stayed in contact. Sometimes sending over 50 letters in the first few days upon arriving at the new prison, Dave was always happy to share that he was one step closer to leaving his gated community, as he jokingly calls it.

"Still, knowing that everyone I cared about was doing the time with me was a constant challenge," Dave said. "There is no way to make being incarcerated seem okay, seem like just another day, or seem like it might even be a positive experience. When I would read the letters before sending them out in the mail, I would hope that my positive words seemed sincere and not some thinly veiled attempt to pretend I was not being ground down by the experience."

Dave wrote letters to remind himself of his individuality.

"Basically, I wrote to let them know that I was still the David Suro that they know, and that being #166054 was just a temporary set-back that I was determined to have as small an effect on me as possible," Dave said. "I was happy when people would write to me and ask me for advice about one thing or another. To be able to be of some service to people in my life was wonderful. It didn't happen very often, but when it did, it reminded me of who I was in their eyes: a son, a brother, a nephew, a cousin, and a friend."

While Dave served his sentence, life continued beyond the walls. Dave left belongings in his father's basement. His father had shared that house with Dave's mother before she passed away. During the first fall of Dave's incarceration, his dad met someone from his church and they were married within six months. Dave's father sold the house, hosting a garage sale, which included Dave's personals stored in the basement. Dave knew that his father sold his belongings for cheap rates because a fist fight broke out over the merchandise.

"I can't complain," Dave joked. "My dad treated me really well while I was incarcerated."

I met Dave's aunt and uncle, Roger and Donna Suro, on a FaceTime call. They live on the east coast. They were enthusiastic about the book and seemed light-hearted in nature. Roger told me that one of the funniest things Dave told him while in prison was that he lived in a gated community. In spite of Dave's intelligence, Roger quipped, he always found himself in weird situations, such as the time he participated in naked relays at his college.

I had to grill Dave about this.

The University of Florida track team held a racing event in the middle of the night; all participants were naked. The event culminated in a group of 50 athletes running around a golf course.

"I think there may have been children conceived at some of those events," Dave laughed.

Roger told me about Dave's days as a physical education teacher who lived in a trailer with no facilities. He took showers in the coach's office to save money.

"He just wanted to coast and have a good time," Roger said. "He was always the goofball and silly, even though he was brilliant. He's so smart he doesn't have any common sense."

Roger also describes Dave as someone who would rather lay in the sand at the beach than use nice beach chairs.

"He's just nuts," Roger said. "It would make me laugh all the time."

Donna thinks that it may have been difficult for Dave to grow up in his older brother's shadow; his brother, like their father, became a successful military pilot.

When Donna and Roger first got news that Dave was going to prison, they were shocked and full of sorrow about his sentence.

"We felt that he got way more than he should have gotten," Donna said. "He deserved to do something but not what they gave him."

Donna was quite surprised that Dave never developed a victim mentality and didn't succumb to depression. When Roger and Donna visited Dave en route to a ski trip, they were surprised they couldn't touch him. They were also surrounded by people who were different than they had experienced before. They chatted with the officers in charge of the visiting room, who offered positive comments about Dave. While they visited, Dave ate vending machine snacks and they joked about how some guards did nothing but drive around the perfectly manicured grounds looking for escapees. They were surprised to see Dave had put on some muscle—he didn't look as much like a beanpole, Donna said.

Roger asked a former judge from Delaware with whom he played poker about Dave's situation. The judge told Roger that if the incident happened in Delaware, Dave would be out on probation. Roger thinks the difference in sentencing between states is a result of Colorado having elected judges, which results in differing punishments. Roger believes judges feel pressure to demonstrate their tough-on-crime credentials and rely on appeals to reduce the sentences later. Donna thinks that Dave's prison behavior led to his early release.

Now that he's out, Donna mourns what he could have achieved if not for the prison sentence or the labels and restrictions associated with it.

"When you look at him you see the education that he's had and his life is kinda ruined in a way, can't ever practice," Donna said. "It's sad. I just can't imagine if it was my son. I'm pleased that he's making every effort to do something with his life because he's actually one of the luckier ones getting out of prison."

We talked about how lucky he was to have funds to start up a business, compared to the many who leave prison with nothing but oversized prison pants and foam flip flops. On the day of his release, Dave's dad picked him up from prison and bought him new clothes and shoes.

Roger wondered what other men did upon their release. Dave taught me that most have almost no choice but to contact the old friends with whom they got into trouble before. I told Roger this.

"I never gave that a thought," Roger said. "It's kinda sad. I feel sorry for convicts when they get out."

I spoke with Dave's cousin, Beth Champe, over FaceTime. She is a warm person with an affinity for Star Wars. Her mother and Dave's mother were twins.

"What I remember of Dave and what I know of Dave is he's very smart and very funny and very sensitive," Beth said. "We always got along great as kids. We get along great now. I try and keep in touch with him as best I can. He's very complex, so I don't want to oversimplify him, but he's very considerate, kind, funny, and way smart. I always looked forward to getting together with all the cousins because it was always a good time with us all hanging out. We would play games. We would play action figures. We would go to amusement parks. We would play music. We just always had a good time together."

Throughout Dave's prison sentence, Beth supported him unequivocally.

"I was saddened by it because I knew he had been struggling a lot during that time," Beth said. "I wasn't exactly sure what happened. I really don't know all the details, and it doesn't matter to me because I supported him. It didn't change my opinion of him in any way. I did what I could to offer support from the outside as best I could. It was still the same Dave that I knew and remembered. As far as his tone and how he saw things, he put an optimistic spin on it as best as he could."

Beth was excited upon Dave's release. She thought he could finally exhale from the whole experience, and maybe she could exhale with him.

"I was always concerned that he would get hurt or that someone would hurt him in there," Beth said. "I understand that didn't really happen. He was able to get along with people and not have any of those problems. He was just making the best of the situation."

Beth began to cry during the interview and apologized for getting emotional. I was touched by the abiding bond between them. I couldn't imagine how hard it would be to have a close family member in prison.

"I love Dave," Beth said. "Dave is like a brother to me, so I'm really glad that he's out. It's more than just a cousin who lives in another state."

She looks forward to seeing him for the first time since he's been out.

"The hardest part of my incarceration was knowing that everyone in the world who I cared about would be affected, and most likely in a negative way to some extent," Dave said. "I was confident that I would be able to get through my sentence, though I knew that there would be times that wouldn't be easy. After all, I had survived every other challenge that life had presented. What I didn't know how to do, though, was make it possible for my sentence to affect me and only me. It's not possible."

Beyond Dave's personal experience, he was well-aware of the toll incarceration inflicted on many families.

Bryan was a career, low-level meth dealer from the Western Slope. He taught Dave the dictum that no drug dealer should involve more than five people in their business. The involved parties should be the dealer, the person from whom he purchases his supply, and three buyers.

Unfortunately for Bryan, his three buyers weren't tight-lipped.

When faced with long prison sentences after their arrests, the buyers snitched on Bryan rather than taking the proverbial

Bryan

fall. So, Bryan began life on the installment plan, leaving a wife and two children behind. His wife had her own meth abuse issues and offered sexual services to feed her addiction. Their children came second. Dave told me that this is a common story he heard from others in prison.

Dave read Bryan letters from the courts regarding his family. Bryan was functionally illiterate. One day a letter came from family court. These letters rarely held good news. With explicit permission from Dave's cellie, Bryan sat on his bed. At 6'4," Bryan weighed 250 pounds. Each man sat on the twin-sized bunks, knees almost touching in the small cell. Dave remembers the letter resting on his lap. Bryan held his head in his hands, his elbows resting on his knees. The letter explained that a STING operation exposed Bryan's wife, who was presently serving a sentence in county jail. His children, ages seven and four, became wards of the state; they would eventually become foster children. The letter also explained that there would be an effort to keep them together. There was no guarantee that the children would even remain in the same city, much less the same house. The grandparents failed to meet the requirements necessary to be caregivers.

"I did my best to remain emotionless as I read the letter," Dave told me. "I just focused on reading one word at a time as the tragic story went from the paper to my eyes and out of my mouth. I tried to turn my brain off and just pretend I was nothing more than a voice recorder set on play. But, I couldn't."

After Dave finished, Bryan had a multitude of questions, as most of the language was legal in nature.

"How do you tell a friend that it means the government is taking his kids from him and that there is nothing he can do or say to make that not happen?" Dave wondered. "How do you tell a friend that it is his own fault for being a meth-dealer and getting wrapped-up over and over, again? How do you tell a friend that it is his wife's fault for being an addict prostitute and abandoning her kids in a car while she goes into a trap-house to turn a $20 trick for another quick high? The only answer I had was to just stick to the basic facts in the letter. I told him that his kids were going into foster care and that the state was going to provide for them as best it could."

A photo of Bryan taken at Delta that he sent out to his family.

Dave's emotions were a jumbled mess.

"I was overcome with worry for the future of those children," Dave said. "I was overcome with frustration for the blight that drugs bring onto our society. I was overcome with sadness as I watched the tears dripping to the floor from the eyes of my broken friend who sat only a foot in front of me. I was overcome with anger that this bombshell of a letter had been placed into my hands and that it was me who had to break the news to Bryan."

Bryan asked if Dave could help. Dave felt useless when he had to tell him no.

"The truth is that there was absolutely nothing I could do, nor anyone else, to change the events that were already in place," Dave said. "The silence following that syllable was so complete that I could hear his tears as they hit the carpet at his feet."

They sat like that for a few minutes, with heads hung low. Dave offered to pray for Bryan's family even though Bryan never prayed. Dave offered the room for as long as Bryan needed to collect himself. Dave didn't want him facing the crowded day room with red eyes.

"I got up, put on my sunglasses, ball-cap, and watch and left the building to walk the yard with purpose," Dave said. "Once I got to the lower part of the camp, down where there were rarely any other inmates walking around, I stopped and allowed my own tears to flow."

The Word on the Yard

"In the beginning was the Word, and the Word was with God, and the Word was God."

John 1:1

Guys from different living units converged on the yard, an outdoor recreational area. It was a space to settle debts, pass contraband, and, most importantly, gossip. If cops shut down the facility, inmates were locked in their cells not knowing why. Following lockdown days, the yard was abuzz with information. Many were curious, although some gang shot-callers wanted reprisal fights in retaliation for the initial rumbles that caused the lockdown.

"For a guy like me, the day after a lockdown was always a time of curiosity," Dave told me. "I would like to know what had occurred, so I knew who to stay away from. Since I had buddies in each of the gangs, I wanted to know which gangs were involved, so I could keep a safe—but polite—distance while everything was sorted out between them. One thing that I was concerned about was being in the wrong place at the wrong time and getting mixed up in a ten-on-ten mini-riot. They were extremely violent and ugly events."

The gossip passed on the yard was called "the word on the yard." By prefacing a comment with "the word on the yard has it that..." an inmate could talk about the business of other inmates more loosely than normal. Still, names were never mentioned.

"The word on the yard has it that dude in the laundry got busted with other dude's pills and was taken to seg," Dave told me a typical conversation would go. "The word on the yard has it that dude talked to the cops while he was in seg and now other dude got wrapped up. So, other dude's crew handled laundry dude in D-unit and it got ugly."

Despite its vagueness, it was easy to surmise the meaning.

"It was equally easy to know that there would be a ripple effect of violence for the next few days and that spending more time in the library or in my own cell—usually reading or playing Scrabble—would be a good idea," Dave said. "I would avoid going to the gym or the yard until the buzz settled down. Tension was palpable during those times. Everyone walked a little differently, spoke a little less and a lot more quietly, and people who were involved always looked either nervous or angry."

Dave thought about the slang, "the word on the yard," and how it reminded him of the Bible being called "The Word of God," or often just "The Word."

"I thought about how I could be a part of spreading The Word on the yard instead of 'the word on the yard,'" Dave said. "It was a delicate subject because the guys who were walking around ranting and raving about scripture were usually seen in a negative light—no one really liked being subjected to the ramblings of an extroverted preacher."

Dave explained that many overly religious types in prison tended to be child sex offenders, hiding behind a stack of Bibles.

To spread The Word on the yard, Dave practiced the virtues

of politeness and respect. He helped with legal work or read letters from home to guys who were illiterate. With trusted friends, like Sean and Chase, he discussed Bible passages while walking laps.

Reflecting on his five goals set when entering prison, Dave accomplished all of them, he thinks.

"Throughout my time, I was trying to get better at it while at the same time trying not to become good at it because I was fighting against getting the convict mentality," Dave said. "I always tried getting my thoughts more on the streets than in the prison."

Dave views his interactions with difficult COs as a way of helping improve his overall mental and emotional health. His pushback helped him disavow the prisoner label; he knew there was much more to him than his D.O.C. number.

"It was pretty easy for me to be arrogant and push back against the police and be a know-it-all when it came to the rules and stuff like that, but when it came to faith, I always tried to make it as simple as I possibly could," Dave said.

Dave learned big lessons like never praying for personal favors, although there were many he could have prayed for.

"Even when I was up for parole, I never prayed that I would get a favorable outcome with parole," Dave said. "I thought that was pretty pointless. My faith told me God is pretty certain that I want to be paroled."

Dave prayed from a position of gratitude after being paroled. He knew firmly that God was on the side of justice and knew Dave's singular needs.

Dave remembers drawing lessons from Jesus' disciples. Dave believed that the actions he did for others were actually actions he was doing for God.

"That's what we are supposed to do in here is look after each other and give each other a helping hand," Dave said.

———

You Fuck Man and Sharkman

You Fuck Man was Vietnamese and would say "you fuck man" instead of "fuck you." No one knew why he was in prison, and he fell into the "other" racial category of prison culture. He worked on the lawn crew and shoveled snow. You Fuck Man and Sharkman, named for biting a cop during a pat down, once stormed off to fight after arguing over a PlayStation controller. You Fuck Man used his belt and a padlock as a club against Sharkman. Sharkman had him in a chokehold. Sharkman retreated to the bathroom, all bloodied. Knowing Dave was a doctor of sorts, Sharkman arrived at his cell with a wad of toilet paper under his hat, soaking up the blood from his wound. Dave remembers seeing the grooves of the padlock imprinted on Sharkman's head. Dave obtained a needle and thread and stitched up the wound.

"I had no clue what I was doing," Dave said. "This is just a bizarre moment. I don't know what I'm doing. I know how to tie a knot. I know how to sew fabric together. I guess it's pretty much the same thing."

By this point, Dave knew he should remain quiet whenever questioned by a captain. He simply told them that he and Sharkman were having a conversation. My jaw dropped when Dave told me this story. I couldn't believe he had the courage to suture a wound with non-surgical grade materials. Although many believed he missed prison social cues, I sometimes think Dave's perseverance in remaining a social and helpful person resulted in something beautiful. Dave became someone you could rely on not only for legal work, but for medical care. Dave did this without hesitation, knowing that he would have to lie to cops.

Dave fondly remembers working in the kitchen with a

young guy, Money, who was in for dealing cocaine. Money grew up in the drug-dealing lifestyle, with most of his family doing the same type of work. They bonded over trivia questions and sports. Money was glad to be incarcerated because he had taken a generous plea bargain for a six-year sentence instead of the 24-year sentence originally expected. He plans to return to selling cocaine when released.

"I hope he's doing well," Dave said. "I really liked him."

I wonder if Dave would have met someone like Money had he not been to prison. And would the many incarcerated men have met someone like Dave?

I think about how far I have come in my own thinking. No one is a criminal to me anymore, just people. And the roughly 2.2 million people in U.S. prisons all have a story.

———

Anxious on the Outside

Cory

I interviewed Cory last. Unexpectedly released prematurely due to COVID-19, he'd been in and out of prison for the past 10 years for theft and drug charges. He was shocked to be released early.

"I've never seen them push people out and have empty beds," Cory said. "If they have less capacity, then they have less ground to stand on to ask for more in their budget."

Although very little of the funding actually goes toward the inmates.

"The criminal justice system is not about justice or restoration," Cory said.

Cory broke into a car and fell asleep, resulting in his most recent prison stay. He woke up to guns in his face. Police officers almost shot him.

"It's not about restoration or making reparations," Cory said. "I did $312 worth of damage to the vehicle. It would have taken me less than a week just to repay because a person doesn't care if I go to jail. They care if their car gets fixed. That's the most important part."

The prosecutors first offered to give Cory a minimum sentence of 36 years because of prior convictions. It was then lowered to a 24-year sentence.

Cory utilized the law library and appealed his sentence, reducing it to 15 months. Had he not familiarized himself with the legal system, he would still be in prison for years to come.

Cory met Dave in the day room of their living unit at Sterling. He explained to another guy where the sciatica nerve is and how to stretch it. Dave was impressed with his accurate description and later helped Cory adjust his five dislocated ribs into place.

"Dave is not one of us," Cory said. "I was a bad guy, did all the bad guy things. Dave's there, but he doesn't belong there, if that makes sense. He comes from a whole different walk of life. When you do enough time locked up, you hear the same stories. Everybody is walking around with their chest puffed up. Everybody is trying to peacock. Everybody's the toughest dude.

Everybody's the biggest drug dealer. Everybody's is the most of this. When you do a lot of time, you learn to just tune a bunch of the stuff out."

For Cory, Dave stood out.

"So, when people come along that are unique, they have unique thoughts and perspectives and backgrounds," Cory said. "You think you might get along with this dude. He's not acting the same way. Different is good. You get tired of hearing the same story."

Cory also talked about Dave's competitive streak, including his propensity for memorizing two-letter words to win Scrabble games and his love for the Tour de France. Cory and Dave loved people watching on the yard over cups of coffee.

Cory, a man of many talents, playing the cello.

"When you're in a box, you don't have a lot of options other than look and dissect yourself," Cory said. "It's the darker side of life. Not a lot of people know about the dark side of life. They want to pretend like they do, but they just don't know."

Cory explained that many people in prison rely on their physicality to win arguments. He thinks that this tendency might be due to people's lack of education; they know no other way to respond. He knew that Dave couldn't approach prison life with such an attitude. Cory is impressed that Dave still found ways to interact with others, in spite of a lack of common ground.

"When you go to prison, you become an object," Cory said. "They strip all your humanity away. You get naked all the time. You show your junk to random-ass people all the time because they tell you to do it. And if you don't, then they respond with force. That's the bar that they set. You do what I tell you to do and if you don't, then you're going to get messed up, but on the same token, we don't want you to act like that. It doesn't work."

Cory struggles with life outside of prison. He told me about the year he spent in a halfway house after his last prison release.

"It was probably the best I ever did," Cory said.

He asked not to be released from the house. He was doing well, making about $50,000 a year in a management position. He didn't want things to change.

"I had too much free time, and it all came unraveled pretty quick," Cory said. "What do I do? The first time I don't have anything to push against, because my life gets so unbalanced because of these things."

It's hard for Cory to cope outside of prison. He told me that prison gives people something to push against all the time. He misses that.

"Prison is a place of extremes," Cory said. "On the one hand, you have people that have no conflict resolution skills at all. They can't heal anything and they only have one or two avenues that they go and they're all super violent. Imagine never getting away from the same 100 people for years of your life. You're just stuck."

He told me living with the same guys forced him to deal with any issues that arose. Avoidance was impossible. Outside of prison, there are many variables.

"All of the unknowns give me super anxiety," Cory said.

Among Cory's multitude of worries, he wasn't certain if he could find a good enough job because of COVID.

"I have my moments when it's just easier to go back to prison," Cory joked. "Where's the instruction guide to this shit? I don't necessarily want to do the things that landed me in prison, but just being there I understand the social dynamics."

Cory now lives with his son. He's not used to familial intimacy.

Cory explained that he isolates frequently and doesn't want to see his mistakes reflected in others' expressions.

"So, I just go somewhere else where I don't have to be around it," Cory said. "Because of that, I've done a lot of damage to my familial ties. I've done a lot of damage to relationships. I look back and here's this wake of chaos."

Cory said that he has moments of brokenness in his head.

"I haven't gotten the balance part of yet," Cory said. "I'm still working on it."

———

Dave's Release

Dave brought his prison ID to one of our meetings. He looked less than enthusiastic in the picture. Taken the day before his release, there was a miscommunication regarding his parole officer. Once resolved, Dave transported his belongings in a large shopping cart. A cop dug through the shopping cart, surveying the letters and other personals. He also charged Dave for a seven-dollar t-shirt. Despite the hassle, Dave's dad picked him up.

Now Dave lives a simple life. He rents a small apartment and volunteers at a food bank every week. He's focused on taking everything one day at a time. Dave prides himself on having thick skin.

"I will always carry the stigma of being a convicted violent felon," Dave said. "And when I tried to get an apartment, that became very clear. And when I tried to get a background check for a job stocking shelves at Home Depot."

But stigmas haven't stopped Dave.

"I'm kind of a pragmatic thinker," Dave said. "I'm very patriotic. I say, okay, well this is America. I don't have to get a job. I can go make a job. I can buy a beat-up pick-up truck. I've got some saws and things. I can go trim trees. I can frankly make a much better living than I would have stocking shelves. Never once have I gone to somebody's house to bid on doing tree work, and they say okay, we're going to have to run a background check on you just to make sure."

Dave drives around in his old Ford truck. The bed is decked out with tree equipment. The sign on his truck reads: "no job too small, some are too big."

I smile when I see it. I hope the world does too.

About the Author

Zoë Jennings is a young writer. She earned degrees in journalism and history from Colorado State University. She wrote and edited for the arts and culture desk of the Collegian, the university's newspaper. Though she has been writing all her life, *The Word on the Yard* is her first book. She enjoyed writing articles with her journalism background, but knew that writing a book would give her time to deeply explore a subject. She is a firm believer that everyone has a story. She looks forward to telling those stories in future projects. When she's not writing, she's teaching preschoolers, doing yoga, kayaking, or hiking.

About the Author

David Suro is a former inmate who spent almost five years in the Colorado Department of Corrections prison system. Since his release in 2019, Dave has been focusing his efforts on prison reform by working as a legal consultant. He also works as a motivational speaker by sharing his experiences as an inmate and encouraging others to overcome challenges in their own lives.

Made in the USA
Columbia, SC
10 June 2021

39671855R00088